D1596443

Broken Three Times

A STORY OF CHILD ABUSE IN AMERICA

Joan Kaufman, Ph.D.

OXFORD
UNIVERSITY PRESS

OXFORD
UNIVERSITY PRESS

Oxford University Press is a department of the University of Oxford. It furthers
the University's objective of excellence in research, scholarship, and education
by publishing worldwide.Oxford is a registered trade mark of Oxford University
Press in the UK and certain other countries.

Published in the United States of America by Oxford University Press
198 Madison Avenue, New York, NY 10016, United States of America.

© Oxford University Press 2016

First Edition published in 2016

Library of Congress Cataloging-in-Publication Data
Kaufman, Joan.
Broken three times : a story of child abuse in America / Joan Kaufman.
    pages cm
Includes bibliographical references and index.
ISBN 978-0-19-939915-4 (hardback)
1. Child welfare—United States—Case studies.   I. Title.
HV741.K378 2016
362.760973—dc23
2015033656

This book is dedicated to the three individuals portrayed in this story, and the countless others like them whose story never gets told. I am grateful to the individuals depicted as Maria, Samya, and Sylar in this book for their courage in allowing me to put in writing what they long to forget. Fifty percent of the profits from this book will go to the three of them; I hope it is enough to make an iota of a difference in their lives.

CONTENTS

PREFACE

Fucked up.

Those are the words Samya uses to describe the child welfare system that served as her legal guardian from age 12 to 17.

Broken is the term I prefer. Or the term I used to prefer up until the last few years when the child welfare system in Connecticut and many places nationwide began a series of innovative reforms that are making Samya and her family's story a thing of the past. Budget cuts have decimated the child welfare system in several other states though, so *broken* is still a term that unfortunately applies in far too many jurisdictions.

I met Samya, her brother, and mother when I was conducting a study to evaluate an intervention developed for children removed from their parents' care due to allegations of abuse or neglect. Samya and her brother also participated in two other research studies I conducted, including a study of genetic and environmental modifiers of depression in maltreated children, and a brain imaging study for children with Posttraumatic Stress Disorder (PTSD).

This book is a biographical, narrative nonfiction retelling of this family's saga. It was written after reviewing our research files, multiple psychiatric hospitalization reports, and almost 1,800 pages of child welfare records. I visited many of the places Samya and her family lived over the years, and conducted numerous interviews with Samya, her brother, mother, former foster parents, therapists, and mentors. The facts are real, and some of the dialogue has been extracted directly from the case record. Some scene and setting details, however, were added to keep the story engaging.

This book also provides brief policy analyses and practice updates, with various incidents of the family's story providing a launching point for discussing emerging trends. It also includes a discussion of advances in neuroscience and genetics relevant for understanding risk and promoting resilience in maltreated children. The book provides an understanding of the complexity of the issues involved with child welfare, ideas about concrete steps to take to improve practice, gaps in our knowledge, and a deepening appreciation of the value of incorporating broad perspectives into this work—from neurobiology to social policy.

To protect the family's confidentiality, the names of all the characters in this book have been changed, as have the names of the cities and towns. Samya is not the real name of the girl in this story. It is a name of Arabic origin that means "on high, exalted," and it is the name the real girl in this story chose for her character. In addition, the family did not originally come from New York, but rather another neighboring state.

I usually write academic papers, but chose to write this book to bring to life the problems of parents and children involved with child welfare—the system set up in this country to deal with cases of child abuse and neglect. In my 25 years of experience working in this field, I repeatedly saw the pain and suffering of children *and* parents exacerbated by flaws in the system. Far too often parents and children do not receive the mental health and addiction services they need, siblings are separated from one another and moved for capricious reasons, and children grow up in institutions, disconnected from their families, with no real supports to call their own. Although this is the story of one family, it unfortunately typifies countless others.

As noted earlier, from the time I started this book to today, child welfare systems in many states have started a process of significant reforms. Trauma-informed systems of care, differential response teams, and strengthening of community-based mental health and addiction services are just a few trends that have begun to transform the system. Time will tell whether these reforms will be sustained, expanded and achieve the desired results.

My impetus to write this book, however, also arose from personal circumstances. After a change in the administration of the Connecticut child welfare leadership, a moratorium was imposed on my research in August 2006. The moratorium not only prevented the recruitment of maltreated children and the collection of DNA specimens for a federally funded research study for more than five years, it prohibited further characterization of our stored DNA specimens, and limited the analyses and publications we were allowed to complete on data we originally had permission to collect. Our science was completely stalled, hijacked.

I do not profess to understand fully all the forces that led to the moratorium after years of productive collaboration with the State. Parents of other special needs populations, through organizations like Autism Speaks and the Juvenile Bipolar Foundation, clamor for state of the art biomedical research to help improve the developmental trajectory of their children. Among child welfare administrators who serve as surrogate parents for children involved in child welfare, there were concerns that our genetics research would stigmatize minorities who are overrepresented in the system, and biomedical perspectives would overshadow the importance of social factors in the conceptualization of the problems and search for solutions to ameliorate risk.

Polarized thinking about the role of genetics and environment, however, is passé. Emerging research suggests the line between social and biological factors has become entirely blurred, and social experiences can alter gene expression. This is a topic I will discuss further later in this book.

Fortunately, there appears to be growing appreciation in the field that insights achieved in the biomedical sciences can inform and improve child welfare practice. I was recently asked by Bryan Samuels, the former Commissioner for the Administration on Children, Youth and Families, the federal agency that oversees all state child welfare services, to participate in two conferences: one on Child Maltreatment and Neuroscience, and a second on Mental Health Consequences of Exposure to Violence, Trauma, and Toxic Stress. Central to the themes of both meetings was the relevance of advances in neuroscience in informing social policy and improving the developmental trajectory of vulnerable children. We also recently have been granted permission to reinitiate our multidisciplinary program of research, albeit outside of Connecticut, in a different jurisdiction.

In writing this book, I have tried to achieve a balance between presenting the reader with the raw and harsh realities of Samya and her family's life, and discussing emerging policy trends and scientific insights that hold significant promise for improving the experience and outcomes of the next generation of children and families to be served by the system.

Maria is the name the mother in this family chose for her character in this book. Like many mothers involved with child welfare, she was addicted to crack cocaine at the time her children entered care. The first time I met Maria, I supervised a visit between her and Samya and Samya's brother, Sylar. Maria defied my stereotyped expectations. She had long beautiful African braids and a Cheshire cat smile that radiated when she talked with her children. There was a rhythm and ease in the way they related to one another—that I have to confess, I only sometimes experience with my own "normal" family.

This family, and Sylar in particular, remained in the forefront of my mind throughout the years for two reasons. Firstly, a staff member who worked with me took the photo of him that is depicted on the following page and illustrated on the cover of this book. It was taken at a quiet moment at the day camp he attended where many of the assessments for our research were completed. He was waiting for the bus back to the foster home where he was living at the time he attended our summer program. It is among the photographs I frequently show when presenting our research data. The picture is artistically framed, the setting peaceful, the colors cheerful, but the sadness of his demeanor still stabs me today when I look at this photo, even though I have seen it more times than I can count.

The second memory that stands out for me about Sylar comes from a conversation I had with one of my research associates, Heather, after she completed a follow-up interview with Sylar six months after our summer camp program. He had been in the system just under ten months at the time, and was already in his fifth placement. As part of the follow-up assessments Heather completed a social-support interview. She asked him to name the people he talked to about personal and private things, who he turned to when he needed advice, who he shared news with when something really good happened, and other

Sylar at our research summer day camp program awaiting a bus to his foster home.

general questions regarding support. One of the camp counselors from our summer program emerged as Sylar's top support, and the other two counselors who worked with him at our camp emerged high on his list of supports. Although I was glad he had positive memories of our staff, his naming them told me he really did not have anyone he could count on. He only knew these counselors for one week and had not seen or spoken to them in the six months since camp ended.

He was drowning.

I was never involved in this family's direct clinical care. I was mostly just an outside observer during the years the family was involved with the child welfare system. I got updates from Heather when she did follow-up assessments;

and I had the opportunity to see both Sylar and Samya when they came to Yale to participate in one of our neuroimaging studies. What struck me most about both of them then, was how their manners topped the etiquette of most children in my own children's elite private schools. Speaking with them and interacting with them, one would never know all they had been through.

In the process of working on this project, however, I have come to know Maria, Sylar, and Samya quite well. One evening, about two years into working on this project, I got a phone call from Maria on my cell phone. She had some news about Sylar that she wanted to share. Before she got off the phone, she asked if I minded that she called to tell me the news. She then added, "It's just that you're like family now, and I wanted to let you know."

I was glad she thought to call. It has been a privilege to work on this book with this family. I have learned a lot. *Broken Three Times* is a book about broken promises, broken spirits, and the broken child welfare system that nearly broke the three individuals portrayed in this story. I am hopeful that the telling of their tale will be an impetus for ongoing positive and permanent change in the system, as well as a deepening appreciation of the value of incorporating broad perspectives into this work—from neurobiology to social policy.

ACKNOWLEDGMENTS

I am grateful to the National Institutes of Health for their funding of our studies, their commitment to ongoing research with this vulnerable population, and their support during the long moratorium on our work. I also want to acknowledge the State of Connecticut Department of Children and Families (DCF), as well as the State of Vermont DCF, who have allowed our science to flourish, and acknowledge the numerous children and parents I have worked with who have touched my life and taught me immeasurable lessons over the years. Beyond this, I am indebted to my grandmother, parents, husband, and children who have given me the support and freedom to follow my professional pursuits.

Broken Three Times

1

1975

The Snoopy Snow Cone Machine

The late afternoon sunlight streams in through the living room window while Scooby Doo plays on the television. Maria nestles into her older sister Tina's side, and Tina's arm is wrapped around her as they cuddle on the overstuffed sofa. The brightly colored clips at the end of each of Maria's braids spray in an array of different directions and bounce each time she laughs.

"Is mom coming home soon?" Maria asks.

"She should be off shift and home in a bit."

At 16, Tina is 10 years older than Maria, and like a second mother to her.

When a key turns in the door to the apartment, Maria and Tina avert their attention from the TV and toward the doorway. There is a minute delay before the door opens so Maria looks up at Tina, awaiting a cue.

Their mother eventually comes into the apartment; her white uniform wrinkled from a long day at the hospital. She leaves her coat and bag by the front door, walks to the couch, gives them each a kiss on the tops of their heads, and plops deep into the green cushy recliner beside them.

Their mom puts her head back and closes her eyes for a minute. She then sits up and asks, "You guys don't need me to cook dinner for you tonight, do you?"

Without waiting for an answer their mother pulls herself up out of the recliner and heads toward the kitchen.

"When this cartoon is over, you two come in the kitchen to help me, okay?"

Maria and Tina agree. When the episode is over they shut off the television and go to the kitchen. Tina turns on the small radio that rests on the window ledge. "Get Down Tonight," by KC & The Sunshine Band, is playing. The three of them sing with the radio, and Tina and Maria dance as they move about the kitchen. Each time Tina bumps Maria on the hip, Maria pretends to fall down, then immediately gets up eager for her big sister to bump her again.

"Lady," by Styx, comes on next. Tina and her mom let Maria sing a solo. They lean against the counter to watch Maria in full form as she belts out the lyrics. Maria knows the lyrics to almost all the popular songs, even though she is only a first grader. When Maria performs she looks like a young Diana Ross, and one can guess that as she is singing, she is imagining herself a pop star on a stage with scores of adoring fans.

After finishing her solo and taking a few bows, Maria sets the table. She has Tina check to make sure she put everything in the right place and her big eyes sparkle when she gets her sister's seal of approval.

The sound of crackling oil and the smell of fried chicken fill the air, reminding them all how hungry they are. But just before dinner is ready, Maria's dad thunders through the door.

"Where the fuck is my dinner?"

The smell of moonshine permeates the room. Whenever he smells like this, things get nasty.

Tina gets Maria from where she stands wide-eyed and frozen by the dining room table. She takes Maria by the hand and leads her back to her room, keeping her eyes on her dad as she cautiously walks away from the crossfire. Through the thin walls they hear the shouts. Tina reads to Maria while they huddle in her bed, and they stay in Tina's room for the remainder of the night.

The next night when Maria's dad comes home he is buoyant. He walks into the apartment holding a huge bag behind his back. "I have a surprise for you," he calls out in a singsong voice.

Maria bounces up and runs across the room to where her dad has put down a big white *Toys R Us* bag. Her heart cries out as she looks at the brightly colored letters on the bag. She cannot wait to see what's inside. Just as Maria is about to open the bag, she hears the plastic crinkle, and whish, the bag is gone. Her dad has lifted it over her head and started carrying it toward the kitchen. Maria follows eagerly behind.

Her mom and sister come into the kitchen to see what all the commotion is about. At last her dad reveals the contents of the bag—it is a Snoopy Snow Cone Machine! Every time the commercial came on the TV, Maria said she wanted the Snoopy Snow Cone Machine; she cannot believe she has one! Maria carefully opens the aqua blue box and asks her dad to put the machine together.

Maria's mother looks at the clock on the wall. It is almost time for Maria to go to bed. She knows by the excitement in Maria's eyes that there is no way she will go to bed without trying her new snow cone machine. Maria's mother and Tina leave the kitchen, and not a word is said about the late hour or Maria's need to get up early for school the next day.

Maria looks at the pictures on the box while her dad puts the pieces of the snow cone machine together, her legs swinging and dangling under her chair while she waits. She helps by cleaning up; throwing out the plastic bags that contained each piece, and setting up the paper cups and other supplies along the edge of the table.

In no time, it is assembled. Her Snoopy Snow Cone Machine looks just like the one on TV! It is shaped like Snoopy's doghouse, white with a red roof and pictures of Charlie Brown and Lucy surrounding the front door. Snoopy sits atop the chimney wearing a long red stocking hat. Maria cannot wait to make her first snow cone!

Step One. Put the packet of red cherry flavor-aid in a bowl with one cup of water and one cup of sugar. Her dad allows her to put in some extra sugar and Maria tastes it to be sure it is perfect. It is perfect.

Step Two. Empty the mixture into the Snoopy figure. Snoopy's long red stocking hat unscrews revealing a secret container for the yummy cherry flavor-aid. The opening is small, so her dad has to do this step. A little syrup drips on his finger and he lets Maria lick it clean.

Step Three. Put an ice cube down the chimney and turn the crank on the back of the doghouse. Twenty-five rotations later there are enough shaved ice flakes to fill the first paper snow cone cup. Maria's dad lets her pour the cherry-flavor syrup over the ice.

Maria then puts her snow cone to the side of the table and places an empty paper cup under the opening in front of the doghouse for her dad's snow cone. He puts in another ice cube and begins turning the crank on the back of the doghouse. While he turns it, Maria sings the song from the commercial.

It's yum yum fun and it's cool and clean, and its name is the Snoopy Snow Cone Machine. You drop an ice cube in and get a snow cone out. Yum yum fun is what it's all about.

Her dad sings with her, despite the fact that he does not know all the words and he can barely carry a tune. When her dad's cup is filled with ice shavings, he hands her the Snoopy decanter. She unscrews the red stocking hat and dumps an excess of cherry flavor-aid on her dad's cone, looking up at him and smiling broadly as she does it.

They then grab their paper snow cone cups, tap cones, and say "Cheers."

Yum, is right. Maria circles her tongue around the top of her cone. The ice prickles her tongue, but the sweet taste of the cherry flavored syrup is soothing. Her mouth freezes, but it tastes delicious.

After a few minutes she sticks out her bright red tongue and asks her dad its color. As she does this, a small bit of snow cone drips down the side of her mouth. Her dad leans over and kisses the extra piece of snow cone off her face. Before he pulls back, she feels the warmth of his tongue in her mouth. The contrast of his warm tongue and the cold from the Snoopy snow cone zaps the magic from the air.

Shortly after that, Maria's mom comes in the kitchen and says it's time to clean up and get changed for bed. Maria has a knot in her stomach; she is ready for bed.

A few weeks later, Maria finds herself up late. Her dad had gone out before she went to bed. She is snuggling the stuffy her dad gave her the night before, but she cannot fall asleep.

As she lays awake in bed, she hears him come back in through the apartment door. Her heart accelerates when she hears a crash as one of the dining room chairs falls over. Her mother and sister seem to be asleep. Maria lies still in bed listening as she hears her father rummaging around the house.

After a bit she hears the creak of her door opening. The smell of moonshine is suffocating. She closes her eyes tight and pretends to sleep. She then feels the weight of her father on her mattress and a cold cylinder-shaped object on the side of her head. Next she hears a clicking sound that is all too familiar. Her father has his .38 caliber gun and he has cocked it, like she has heard him do numerous times before while pointing it toward her mother.

She hears him tell her that he loves her. She hears him tell her that he will kill her if she tells anyone this secret. She feels the weight of his body on top of hers, and she feels a burning between her legs. She feels a tear roll off the side of her face, all the while conscious of the sick smell of moonshine.

She opens her eyes and looks past her father to the ceiling above her bed. There are 10 tiles across. The one right above her bed is cracked. The weight of her father makes it hard to breathe. She feels another tear roll down her cheek. The crack in the tile above her bed looks like the Mississippi River on the map her teacher showed her class in school. Another tear runs down her cheek. The tile next to the one with the Mississippi River also has a crack. She cannot decide what that one looks like.

At some point that night her father leaves her room. At some other point that night Maria finally falls asleep.

The next day when Maria wakes up she thinks the encounter with her father was just a bad dream, but as she tries to get up off her bed, the pain in her groin lets her know it was real.

Trauma Informed Systems of Care

Although it has been acknowledged for decades that parents involved with the child welfare system have high rates of childhood trauma,[1] it is only within the past five to ten years that this knowledge has started to shape practice. Emerging data now suggest that when mental health and child welfare systems do not appropriately assess, identify, and address underlying trauma issues, services are often more expensive and less effective.[2] In 2008, the National Child Traumatic Stress Network released a child welfare toolkit that was updated and rereleased in 2013.[3] It is intended to help states and other jurisdictions incorporate the best science and knowledge about child and family trauma into their casework practice, and help child welfare administrators, supervisors, and workers implement trauma-informed strategies in their daily work. The toolkit includes resources to train administrators, caseworkers, and contracted service providers on the effects of trauma; delineates strategies for universal screening of trauma experiences to be used with parents and children; and promotes the dissemination of evidence-based treatment models to address trauma-related psychiatric problems. Systematic research on the impact of implementing trauma-informed systems of care is limited, but preliminary data suggest it is associated with reduced use of inpatient psychiatric services and with significant cost savings, with the savings greatest in families affected by both child and parent trauma histories.[4] (See Reference 3 for the website to download the National Child Traumatic Stress Network's Trauma-Informed Systems of Care Child Welfare toolkit.)

With an infusion of state, federal, and private foundation dollars, Connecticut has been able to implement a trauma-informed system of care. Administrators, caseworkers, and contracted providers have received training on trauma-informed practices. In addition, learning collaboratives have been created to disseminate evidence-based psychotherapies to treat Posttraumatic Stress Disorder (PTSD) and other trauma-related psychiatric problems in children, including Trauma-Focused Cognitive Behavior Therapy (TF-CBT), the evidence-based treatment with the strongest support. The collaboratives have been able to provide ongoing supervision to help mental health providers administer the treatments with fidelity—as intended by the developers. Although correlation does not imply causality, and other factors may have contributed to the drop, since training providers around the state to assess for and treat PTSD in children began, the number of children in the child welfare system requiring inpatient psychiatric treatment has declined considerably. Prior to the implementation of Connecticut's trauma-informed system of care practices, children in the custody of the State due to abuse or neglect comprised 65% of child psychiatric inpatients.[5] This figure is now down to approximately 30%, cut by more than half.[6]

What do these numbers tell us? First of all, trauma-informed care reduces the need for costly inpatient psychiatric services. But children in the custody of the State due to abuse or neglect comprise only about 1% of the population of children in Connecticut, so abused and neglected children involved with the child welfare system remain at inordinately high risk for significant psychiatric problems serious enough to warrant inpatient hospitalization—a rate about 30 times greater than expected by population estimates.

Maltreated children are at high risk for Posttraumatic Stress Disorder (PTSD), depression, suicidality, and a host of other mental health and medical health problems. Evidence-based treatments like Trauma-Focused Cognitive Behavior Therapy (TF-CBT) work better than other practices, but there is not a treatment in psychiatry that works for all patients with a given mental health condition. It is estimated that approximately one in five children who complete TF-CBT will still have enough symptoms to meet diagnostic criteria for PTSD after the standard three to four months of treatment.[7] We are a long way from knowing what works for whom. In addition, for disorders like major depression, we know individuals with a history of child abuse are more likely to have a persistent course of illness than individuals without a history of early adversity. Individuals with a history of child abuse are also less likely to remit following standard evidence-based pharmacological (e.g., selective serotonin reuptake inhibitor medications like Prozac) or psychotherapeutic (e.g., cognitive behavioral treatment) interventions.[8]

Although individuals with a history of early child abuse and those without it might meet the same laundry list of symptoms required for the diagnosis of major depression, there is emerging evidence that the neurobiological correlates of depression in these two groups of individuals may be different.[9] Understanding the mechanisms involved in the development of depression and other stress-related disorders is key to improving the outcomes of kids and parents involved in the system, at least this is one fundamental belief that has guided my career.

We will have time for more biology later; now let's return to the story of Maria and her children, fast-forwarding from our snapshot of Maria's horrendous childhood to the family's first encounter with Connecticut protective services when Sylar and Samya were preteens.

2

2000
The First Investigation

It is a hot summer day, midafternoon, and more than a decade has passed since Maria left home at the age of 17. The air is stifling. Maria is watching TV with her kids in the living room of their new apartment when she hears an unexpected knock on the door. It startles Maria, and she feels light-headed as she gets up to answer the door.

Maria puts her ear to the door and listens for a minute before unlatching the lock. She then pulls the door back slowly and looks out on the porch. A petite Hispanic woman wearing a blue polyester suit with a black notebook in her hand greets her.

"Ms. Jones?" the woman asks.

"Who's looking for her?"

"My name is Sofia. I am an investigations worker with DCF—the Department of Children and Families. Can I come in?"

Maria is new to Connecticut, but she knows about DCF. DCF is the agency that takes your kids away.

Maria looks back toward the living room and says, "Kids go to your room. We got a visitor and I gotta talk to her in private."

Sylar, a lanky 11-year-old, and Samya, who is one year younger than her brother, turn their heads toward their mother. They can tell by her tone of voice and the look of panic in her eyes that they need to do what she says. They get up. Samya shuts off the TV, and they both walk down the hallway to their room.

Sofia, Maria's first DCF worker (DCF-W1), follows her into the living room. They sit on the brown wool plaid couch, which makes Maria's bare legs itch. While Sofia opens her notebook and shuffles some papers, Maria pulls on the legs of her shorts, looks down at the ground, and fidgets.

No pleasantries or banter about the hot weather are exchanged.

Sofia gets straight to the heart of the matter. "Is there a Mark Bard living here with you?"

Not knowing the reason for the question Maria answers, "Yes, my kids and I are sharing this apartment with him. He's just a friend I met at the shelter."

"Did you know he's a convicted child sex offender?"

Maria knew Mark recently had been released from prison. She states that she did not know why he was locked up.

Sofia lets Maria know that someone called the hotline and said she knew he was a sex offender, and that she was leaving him unsupervised with her children.

Maria again denies knowing Mark was a child sex offender, and she contests the claim that she leaves him alone with her children.

"My children go everywhere with me; I don't leave them with nobody."

After making clear that the Department expects her to protect her children—ask Mark to leave or find a new place to live with her children—Sofia asks a lot of background questions.

Maria reports on the basics. She is 32 years old and unemployed. She receives benefits. She never really worked. Between taking care of the kids and her PTSD—Posttraumatic Stress Disorder—she really cannot handle having a job.

As Maria and Sofia talk, the tone of the meeting changes and Maria finds herself sinking comfortably into the cushions of the couch as the interview progresses.

Maria lets Sofia know she has only lived in the apartment a few weeks. She and the kids moved there from the homeless shelter in town, which is where she met Mark. Before that they had been at a battered women's shelter in New York. They went to the women's shelter when Maria left her husband of six years because the violence was just too much to take.

Sofia asks if her ex-husband is the father of her children.

"Not that ex-husband. My first ex-husband, John; he was my high school sweetheart. We were together two years, but it didn't work out too good. He got in with the wrong crowd and he started smoking crack."

"Does he provide child support? Does he have contact with the children?"

"No. We ain't seen him since Samya was two months old. I am not sure the kids even know who he is or who their father is."

Sofia then asks about Maria's family and supports.

"I really don't have no supports—except my kids."

Maria goes on to explain that she was raised by her grandmother, grandfather, and aunt; and they are all dead now.

It turns out that Maria did not actually ever live with her real mom and dad. Toward the end of elementary school, Maria learned that the man she thought was her father was actually her grandfather. Learning this, however, did not make what he repeatedly did to her any less painful.

Maria also learned that Tina was her aunt, not her sister; and the woman she thought was her mother was actually her grandmother. Maria always considered her grandmother her mother, though.

"Birthing don't make you no real mother."

Maria's real mother was her grandparents' other daughter—Tina's older sister. In late elementary school Maria learned that she was the product of an affair. Her birth mother's husband forced her mother to choose between giving Maria up and ending their marriage. Maria's mother chose to give her up.

Maria let Sofia know her grandmother, grandfather, and aunt all died over the past few years, one after the other—grandma first, granddad a few months later, and her aunt after that. She tells Sofia that her aunt Tina was murdered by her boyfriend in front of a crowd of people who stood by doing nothing while they watched her get killed.

"Saw it, found out about it, watching the evening news on TV."

As she tells Sofia how she learned about Tina's death, Maria stares off into space, her eyes glaze over, and the newsreel replays in her head.

Sofia changes the subject and asks Maria about her real mother and if she has any siblings. Maria looks up at Sofia and explains that she only sees her mother once or twice a year. She says her mother is a drunk. Maria also lets Sofia know she has nine sisters and three brothers, but that they are not close.

Sofia asks Maria if she ever received child protective services when she was living in New York. Maria says, "No."

Sofia then interviews the children separately, and leaves an hour or so later. She is vague about when she will be by again, but unwavering in her expectations. Maria is to ask Mark to leave, or find a new place to live with her children.

Slightly over a month passes from the initial visit by Sofia. When she comes back, it is a classic New England fall day. Sylar is at school and Samya is at home helping Maria pack. Maria is too stressed to handle doing it on her own. They have until four o'clock to be out of the apartment. It will be their fourth move in four months, although it feels like longer since they left Maria's ex- and moved into the battered women's shelter in New York.

Maria and Samya are in the back room folding clothes when there is a knock on the apartment door.

"He said he'd give us until four o'clock to be out of here today. What's he hassling us about now. It's only eleven."

"Ma, we don't even know it's him at the door. Chill. I'll get it."

Samya is thin, has light brown skin, beautiful cat-shaped eyes like her mother, and looks like a young Brandy, the actor and singer. Although Samya is only 10 years old and still several inches shorter than her mother, there are times she seems like the parent in the family.

Samya walks nonchalantly to answer the door; it is Sofia. Samya greets her with a big smile and invites her into the apartment.

Maria comes to see who is at the door.

Before Sofia can say hello, Maria blurts out, "We're being evicted."

Sofia is about to ask Maria the circumstances when Maria cuts her off. Maria goes on to explain, "I paid the landlord's brother who said he usually collects the rent. Gave him $400 cash at the beginning of the month. I asked for a receipt, but he said it wasn't necessary. Now the landlord is saying he never got the money and he wants us out. We got 'til four o'clock this afternoon to be out and we don't have nowhere to go."

Sofia tries to sound calm and reassuring. "The landlord can't just put you out on the street. You've got two children. Even if you are on a month-to-month oral lease, there are steps your landlord has to go through to evict you. He can't just tell you to leave. Did the landlord give you a Notice to Quit?"

"A what? He just told us we gotta be out."

"Give me his name and his number. I'll follow up with him."

Maria grabs her purse, which is on the end table by the couch. She pulls out her wallet, her keys, and assorted papers until she finds a small piece of paper with the landlord's name and number. She then writes the information on a napkin and gives it to Sofia.

Sofia then asks, "Where's Mark?"

Maria and Samya answer in unison, "He's gone."

Maria adds, "I wasn't gonna lose my kids 'cause of him. I don't know who told you guys I knew he was a convicted child sex offender, but he never told me that. He's out and I have no interest in having anything to do with him anymore."

"I am glad you did what you needed to do to protect your kids. You know, another call came in to the hotline about you yesterday. Someone said you were using drugs and you had no food for your kids, but the report was not accepted."

"Who would call up and say something like that? I'm not doin' drugs. We're tight on food, but I'm not doin' drugs. Probably was Mark who called, or his sister who is mad I threw him out."

Sofia gives Maria information about a couple of food pantries and soup kitchens in the area. She also is able to clear things up with the landlord, and makes one more unannounced home visit the following week. The notes in the record from that visit state, "The apartment was clean and organized. The children were clean and appropriately dressed. Mother indicated that she was able to get a food voucher and that she had enough groceries. Worker provided mother with additional donated groceries. Worker advised mother to better manage her money to make sure that they have groceries for the whole month."

Sofia then finalized her investigation and concluded, "This worker has reasonable cause to believe that neglect should not be substantiated. The children did not disclose any information that would lead this worker to believe that the children are being abused or neglected. They indicated that they are not left unsupervised and no one has made any inappropriate advances toward them. Mother does not have any criminal history. No medical concerns at this time with the children." The closing recommendation on Sofia's report was, "No further contact." Maria's case was closed, allegations of neglect were nonconfirmed, and Maria and her children were not provided links to any ongoing services.

Differential Response

Results of a national survey based on administrative data suggest that in 2004, approximately 40% of all *confirmed* cases of child maltreatment did not receive any therapeutic or support services.[10] For these families, the investigation was the only "service" provided. Rates of service provision were even lower for nonconfirmed cases like Maria's, despite the extensive trauma histories and significant needs of these families. Recent data suggest improvement in service delivery among families referred to protective services, with 64% of confirmed cases and 33% of nonconfirmed cases receiving some postresponse services, but the rate of unmet service need continues to be inordinately high.[11]

A research study conducted at approximately the same time Maria first interfaced with the Connecticut DCF also found that the process of confirming or substantiating reports of abuse and neglect is relatively idiosyncratic.[12] In this large follow-up study of over 50,000 first-time referrals to protective services for suspected child maltreatment, cases were found to be equally likely to be rereferred for a second report regardless of whether they were substantiated or not substantiated the first time. About half of all confirmed, and half of all nonconfirmed cases were re-referred to protective services during the four-year follow-up period. One would expect "confirmed" cases to be more likely to be re-referred.

These data have led to changes in the way most protective services agencies nationwide are doing business. To date, approximately two-thirds of states in the United States have implemented Differential Response programs that create a two-tier response to allegations of abuse and neglect.[13] The most severe cases involving injury or imminent risk still involve forensic evaluations, but moderate-to-low-risk cases are referred for family assessments instead. The goal of the contact is no longer a formal determination of abuse or neglect, but rather a determination of whether or not services are needed to strengthen families and promote child well-being. Key to the success of differential response models are links with community service providers and collaborations with families' informal natural supports (e.g., friends, relatives).

Differential response programs are defined by the following practices and goals: (1) use of engagement versus adversarial approaches; (2) creation of services versus surveillance plans; (3) labeling parents as "in need of services or support" instead of as "perpetrators"; (4) voluntary versus mandatory services; and (5) a continuum of possible responses.[14] Concretely, these translate into scheduled appointments to share the focus of the child abuse report with the family, versus unannounced home visits, and into service planning meetings that typically involve child protection service workers, parents, and informal supports. Parents are no longer surprised with the ring of a doorbell, and parents are actually viewed as partners in determining the service needs of their families.

Preliminary data from research conducted on differential response programs suggest child safety is better served by this alternative intervention approach. Families who received differential response family assessments were found to have fewer subsequent maltreatment reports, a longer period of time between rereports, and less severe new reports than families receiving traditional protective services investigative interventions. Differential response interventions also are associated with greater family satisfaction, and most importantly, greater involvement with community services.[14-16] (See Reference 15 for the website to download a report by Casey Family Programs about implementing Differential Response interventions that includes links to excellent resources.)

At this point in time, differential response is considered a "promising practice," not an "evidence-based intervention." There are flaws in the research that make the results of some of the prior studies inconclusive, and there are concerns that the model is not being implemented consistently across sites.[17] There are also concerns about the dichotomy in the literature in describing differential response and standard child protective services interventions. Although mandatory services and identifying a "perpetrator" may be necessary in standard protective service investigations, it has been argued that the family-centered practice principles that underlie differential response interventions represent optimal child welfare practice for both intervention tiers.[18] Engagement, creation of service plans, and utilization of a continuum of possible responses should be standard practice with all families referred to child welfare. The challenge in child welfare is to engage and empower families, while preserving the right to mandate services and remove children to ensure child safety when working collaboratively and voluntarily with families is just not enough.[18]

Differential response is the program du jour in child welfare; other programs have been touted as panaceas in the past.[19] The availability of a full continuum of services to meet families' needs is required for the success of differential response programs, and as was alluded to at the end of Chapter 1, there is much we just do not know about optimizing treatment outcomes of individuals involved with child welfare. In addition, as will become evident as we continue with our story of Maria and her children, first encounters often only present the tip of the iceberg. The depths of issues that families are struggling with may only become evident over time.

3

2001

The Second Investigation

Two months after Maria's first case with the Department of Children and Families (DCF) was closed, Maria, Sylar, and Samya are out of that apartment and back in the shelter system. Move number four was temporarily averted, but it was not avoided altogether.

Maria and her children remain in Connecticut, but this time they move from the city to a small rural area. They move to a town only four blocks long. A good thing about the homeless shelter is the guarantee of three meals a day. A bad thing about the move to the shelter is the need for Sylar and Samya to start at yet another new school. They also all have to share one room.

This shelter is less institutional looking than the last one. It is located in an old white Victorian house with a big wraparound porch. At this shelter, however, there is no quietly sneaking out at night. The floors and stairs creak.

Maria and the children have a room up on the third floor. Their room has one small window and a slanted ceiling. Unlike the quaint look of the exterior of the house, the rooms are furnished like barracks. Their room has a black metal bunk bed, a similarly styled single bed, army-green trunks at the end of each bed, and a clothes rod secured on one wall. Samya convinces Sylar to let her have the top bunk and Maria sleeps in the one single bed.

Most nights while they are living at this shelter, one of two scenes will play out. About half of the time, within an hour of turning the lights off in their room, Sylar and Samya hear their mother unlatch the trunk where she keeps her pipe hidden underneath her clothes. They then hear her rummage through her purse and open her glasses case, where she stashes her white rocks, if she has any. Then they hear the click of a lighter. They frequently fall asleep to the sound of her deep breaths, the popping from the pipe, and a stench that is a cross between burned rubber and peanut brittle.

Other nights after getting her pipe from the trunk, they hear their mother getting dressed, the creaking of the floor as she walks across the room, and the never-quiet-enough opening and closing of the door as she sneaks out. Those are the nights it is hardest to fall asleep. They might doze some, but they cannot really sleep until they once again hear the opening and closing of the door to their room, and the creak of her steps back to her bed.

Mornings at this shelter are also almost always the same scenario. Maria stays in bed until eleven o'clock and Sylar and Samya get themselves up and ready for school. Cathy from across the hall sometimes comes to hurry them along if they are running late. Their mom thinks it was Cathy who called DCF alleging, "...Mother is using crack cocaine in her room while the children sleep.... As a result of her drug use, mother cannot get up with her children in the morning to prepare them for school." The report noted, "The caller performs this task for mother."

Maria's case is assigned to a new worker; there is rarely continuity in worker from one investigation to the next. This time it is a man, Randy (DCF-W2). As part of his investigation, Randy interviews the shelter director, Cathy, Maria, Sylar, and Samya. Maria is reported by the shelter director to be spending time with Timothy K., a known drug dealer who had been kicked out of the shelter a few weeks earlier. Most of the time the kids are not with Maria when she is with Timothy K. Sylar and Samya are not sure which is worse, being with their mom when she is in these situations, or imagining what is going on when she is out and about.

When Randy asks Samya if she has ever seen her mother do drugs, Samya says, "No," while envisioning in her mind the trip they made to the apartment in Hartford with Timothy K. the weekend before. She and Sylar mostly stayed in the back room watching TV. When Samya came out into the hallway to go to the bathroom, she heard Timothy K. giving her mother grief for not being able to pay for her share of the crack. As she walked down the hallway Samya thought, "Mom always has ways she can pay for her drugs." When Samya came back into the hallway, she saw her mother on her knees, with her head in Timothy K's friend's groin.

When Sofia (DCF-W1) had interviewed Maria, Maria denied prior involvement with protective services in New York. Randy, however, formally checks into this and learns Maria did have prior involvement with protective services. He gets the records faxed to him.

He reads the records while sitting in his cubby with the bustle of the office whirling around him. He learns that Maria had another child, Gregory, who was the product of a rape. While pregnant Maria had planned to give the child up for adoption, but was too depressed after his birth to initiate the process.

Maria first came to the attention of protective services in New York when Gregory was four months old, Samya just under a year and a half, and Sylar just over two and a half. Maria had brought Gregory to the hospital because he had a life-threatening respiratory infection.

When Gregory was admitted to the hospital, it was noted that he had been seen in the emergency room (ER) for a broken arm three weeks earlier.

According to hospital records, Maria had missed the follow-up appointment that was scheduled for Gregory in the orthopedic clinic, and in fact, Maria had brought Gregory to only one well-child visit, when he was 10 days old.

The referral to protective services was made after a partially healed rib fracture was detected on an X-ray taken when Gregory was in the intensive care unit. As Randy reads the file he imagines the small four-month-old baby in the ICU in a sterile Plexiglass crib with an IV and a respirator dwarfing his small body.

Although the evidence for the allegation was not clearly noted in the record, and no criminal charges were ever filed, Maria was indicated (e.g., confirmed) in the protective services report for the bone fractures. *Did she actually cause the arm and rib fractures?* Maria was also indicated in the report for the medical neglect of Gregory, and "other" neglect involving Sylar and Samya. Randy is not sure what "other" neglect means.

He reads on. He learns that Gregory spent three months in the hospital, and was then discharged to the care of Maria with ongoing supervision from the Department of Protective Services. Randy wonders why Gregory was returned to Maria, but appreciates "family preservation" was the guiding principle in child welfare services when this incident occurred.

After Gregory's discharge from the hospital, Maria was provided supportive services, including a visiting nurse three times per week and a parent aide six hours per week. After three months, the nurse completed her home visits and reported she found Gregory "very healthy and adjusted." She reported "mother is caring for him [Gregory] appropriately." The protective services social worker also reported, "Mother is very cooperative." She noted this "social worker has witnessed her [Maria's] parenting of her children and it would appear she has utilized the parent aide to the fullest."

A month after these notes were filed, Maria called the Department and asked for the voluntary placement of Gregory. Gregory was then placed in foster care for two months until Maria called and requested his return. Gregory was once more returned to Maria, and a parent aide was again provided for support.

Randy stops reading the record and pauses to think about Gregory's first year of life. During his first four months of life, he sustained two fractures. He then spent three months in the hospital, then four months with his biological mother, followed by two months in foster care, until he was again returned to his biological mother. Randy shakes his head and reads on.

A month after the second time Gregory was returned, Maria again requested Gregory's removal. It was reported in the record that "... she [Maria] said she could not love Gregory the way she knew she should and she was afraid she would hurt him." Gregory never lived with Maria again. Voluntary termination of parental rights was finalized seven months later, and Gregory was adopted.

Randy leans back in his chair and stops and wonders how things turned out for Gregory. Feeling slightly sick to his stomach, he reads on.

The New York child protective services record reported no additional contact with Maria over the next eight years. The year before Maria moved to Connecticut, however, two "Early Warnings" involving Maria were filed. A physician at a neighborhood health clinic filed one that described Maria as a "drug seeker" who frequented emergency rooms and various doctors looking for prescription drugs. A psychiatric hospital physician filed a second "Early Warning" that noted Maria tested positive for cocaine, benzocaine, and opiates. Connecticut does not have "Early Warnings." Randy is not sure what they are, but he thinks maybe they should be renamed "Missed Opportunities," given that they do not appear to have led to any follow-up.

After reading the New York records, Randy questions his department's decision to dismiss and not investigate the report submitted a few months earlier that alleged Maria was using drugs.

During the course of Randy's investigation, the allowed 90-day stay at the homeless shelter elapses. Maria, Sylar, and Samya move in with a female acquaintance Maria met at the shelter. This is move five for the year for Maria, Sylar, and Samya. The apartment is only two blocks from the shelter, which means Sylar and Samya can continue in their same school. They still have to share a room, but at least they are not still sharing a room with their mother, too. Within a few days, however, the acquaintance calls the director of the shelter to complain that Maria is leaving the kids alone and going out without explanation. She also alleges that Maria is actively using crack cocaine and says she is going to ask Maria to move out.

One night before the acquaintance has a chance to ask Maria to leave, Maria goes out with Timothy K. Samya dozes fretfully that night, and it is starting to get light out by the time Samya hears Maria come back to the apartment. Samya peers into the living room and watches as her mother bumps into the coffee table then collapses on the couch. Her hair is disheveled, her shirt is torn, and she has a welt over one eye. Samya gets a wet paper towel and puts it on her mother's forehead. Maria looks up appreciatively at Samya before passing out. Samya sits on the floor, rests her head on the couch, and holds her mother's hand. She, too, eventually falls asleep.

At first Maria claimed Timothy K. raped her, but later she confessed he pummeled her because she smoked the last of his crack when he went to the store to get some beer. Following this incident, Maria, Sylar, and Samya move to a battered woman's shelter in another city in Connecticut about half an hour away. This is Maria, Sylar, and Samya's sixth relocation since leaving Maria's ex-. The children's birth certificates were lost in the move, so it is several weeks before Sylar and Samya can enroll in their new school.

Throughout the investigation, Maria denies drug use. Randy, however, requires Maria to have a substance abuse evaluation and sequential hair analysis. After a month and two no-shows, Maria finally completes the assessment.

She tests positive for cocaine on all three panels of the hair analysis, confirming consistent heavy drug use over the past three months.

Shortly after the drug-test results come in, Randy gets a telephone call from the battered women's shelter director letting him know Maria is at risk of being kicked out of the shelter for violating curfew. The shelter has a 7 PM curfew, and Maria has been in violation of it on multiple occasions.

When Maria is out at night she is spending time with Joseph, a light-skinned biracial male with long dreadlocks, nine years her junior. She met him at the soup kitchen down the street from the Women's Shelter. Maria was not supposed to tell Joseph the location of the women's shelter, but she did.

One night at 1 AM Joseph comes by the shelter, banging on a windowpane looking for Maria, rattling the nerves of most of the other residents at the shelter. Maria leaves with him, slipping out while she assumes Sylar and Samya are sleeping. The children stare in silence from their beds as they watch Maria gather her things and quietly exit the door of their room. They are accustomed to being left alone, but the shelter director is fuming. She calls the child abuse hotline. The shelter director tells the person on the hotline that Maria will not be allowed back in the shelter, and that she recommends someone come and pick up the children.

An hour later, after completing the paperwork necessary to invoke a 96-hour hold for the emergency placement of the children, an on-call worker, Kristin (DCF-W3), arrives at the shelter. She waits in the dining hall while the shelter director goes to get Sylar and Samya from their room. When they hear the turn of the doorknob, they think it is their mother returning. When the shelter director turns on the light, they are not sure what to expect, but their stomachs tell them it is apt to be bad.

"Is our mom okay?" Samya asks in a worried voice.

"As best I know. Come with me down to the dining hall. There is someone who wants to talk with you." The director tries to sound warm and caring, but her patience has been worn thin by Maria's antics, and her voice sounds a bit strained.

The shelter director tells Sylar and Samya it is all right for them to come in their pajamas. They follow her, exchanging glances between themselves as they walk silently down the bright fluorescent-lit hallway toward the back staircase to the dining hall. As they walk, Samya focuses on the sound of their feet on the linoleum floors.

When they enter the dining hall, Kristin notes how composed Sylar appears, and how concerned and worried Samya looks. Kristin smiles and greets them warmly. The children look at her, not sure whether they have met her before. She has come with two hot chocolates and a bag of munchkins from Dunkin Donuts.

Sylar and Samya always remember their manners, and even under these stressful and uncertain circumstances, they both smile and thank Kristin for bringing the treats.

After they settle at the table and the shelter director leaves the room, Kristin explains she is concerned that their mom has not followed through and started the treatment she needs. She says it also seems like their mom is acting erratically, and she says the Department is concerned about their welfare. She then explains that DCF is going to take them into custody and find them a safe place to live.

"Where will we be going?" Sylar asks.

"I'm not sure just yet," Kristin replies.

She adds that they are going to start by going to her office so she can make some calls to find a good place for them to stay. She lets the children know that she has a TV and VCR player in her office, and that they can watch a movie and rest on some couches while she makes the necessary phone calls. Kristin thinks about the couches with wooden armrests and immovable pillows in her office, and she imagines the children will not be very comfortable or able to get much sleep.

Kristin then asks the children some questions about school and music while they finish their hot chocolate. Sylar answers her questions, and asks her if she likes Dragon Ball Z, his favorite TV show.

As Sylar and Kristin talk, Samya stares out the window, glassy-eyed, refusing to blink, not wanting the tears in her eyes to roll down her cheeks. The questions she is too afraid to ask, namely, *How long will we be gone*? and *Is my mom okay?* keep replaying in her head.

After they finish their snack, the worker walks them back to their room and helps them put their clothes in black plastic garbage bags. Sylar and Samya put pants and a shirt on over their pajamas, and put sneakers on their feet without bothering with any socks or laces. The worker carries their clothes; they each carry their schoolbooks in their arms, and follow the worker out to the blue official State of Connecticut car.

On the ride to Kristin's office, the children sit in the back of the car. Sylar leans forward and asks Kristin about the movies she has in her office. Samya leans back and asks Kristin to turn up the radio. Sylar and Kristin's words ricochet around the car. Their conversation is lost on Samya. The song, "Survivor," by Destiny's Child comes on the radio. Samya lets the chorus fill her head, "I'm a survivor, I'm gonna make it, I will survive, keep on survivin'. . . ." She thinks about her mother and her many boyfriends who beat on her, and she hopes her mother is okay. Images of the music video flash in her head. She sees Beyoncé on the raft in the raging waters. Who is she kidding? She's not a survivor. She feels like she is drowning. Before the song is over, the car stops. Samya opens the car door, steps into the blackness of the night and silently follows Kristin and Sylar into the DCF office building.

Substance Abuse and Child Welfare

Before discussing the central focus of this brief treatise, I want to comment briefly on the return of Gregory to the care of Maria after he was discharged from the hospital. Children 0–3 years of age comprise the majority of child fatalities nationally, with over 80% of the fatally abused children nationwide falling within this age range.[20] Young children are also at increased risk of hospitalization for serious injury due to physical abuse, with children 0–1 years old 20 times more likely to be hospitalized for serious injury due to physical abuse than 1–18-year-olds.[21] It is concerning that there is nothing in the case notes to indicate that this level of risk was appreciated by the team that was working with Maria and her three children, who were all under the age of three years when they initially received protective services.

On to the primary topic of this brief treatise: The link between parental substance abuse and child maltreatment is well established.[22] It is estimated that 60%–70% of all substantiated child welfare cases, and 80% or more of parents whose children are placed in foster care, meet diagnostic criteria for a substance use disorder. Among child welfare cases, parental substance abuse is associated with higher rates of child revictimization, greater likelihood of out-of-home placement, longer stays in care, and higher rates of termination of parental rights and child adoption.

In 1998, the U.S. General Accounting Office prepared a report for the U.S. Senate Committee on Finance about the challenges facing foster care agencies serving children whose parents have substance use disorders. The report estimated that for each 100 parents required to receive substance abuse treatment as part of their service plan, 64% complete an intake for services, 50% attend some treatment, but only 13% complete treatment. Although we can point a finger at the addicted parents for not following through with their recommended services, when 87% of the parents are falling through the cracks, as professionals, I think we need to ask ourselves, "What aren't we doing right?"

Over the past decade, the U.S. Department of Health and Human Services, Substance Abuse and Mental Health Services Administration, established a National Center of Substance Abuse and Child Welfare (NCSACW).[23] NCSACW has funded numerous demonstration projects to test various service delivery models aimed at improving substance abuse treatment completion rates among parents involved with the child welfare system. (See Reference 22 for a review of this topic and Reference 23 for the website of the National Center on Substance Abuse and Child Welfare, which includes links for relevant resources, trainings, conferences, and technical assistance.)

Maria participated in a demonstration program that was implemented in Connecticut called Project SAFE (Substance Abuse Family Evaluation).[24] The purpose of Project SAFE was to evaluate parents with potential substance abuse problems, utilize this information to inform decisions about child placement, and provide evaluation results to the court as evidence, if needed. Project SAFE involved (1) establishing a collaborative relationship between the State child protection services agency and the State agency responsible for adult mental health and addiction services; (2) developing and implementing use of a screening tool for protective service workers to determine whether clients needed a specialty substance abuse evaluation; (3) hiring a substance abuse specialist to be housed in each of the regional child protection services offices to consult with workers; and (4) contracting with a statewide behavioral health consortium to provide drug testing, substance abuse assessments, and outpatient treatment—with these contracted services available to augment the publicly funded substance abuse assessment and treatment resources.

Over five years, 5,776 parents involved with Project SAFE were referred for a substance abuse evaluation, and intakes were completed on 88% of those referred for specialty substance abuse assessments. This represents a notable improvement over the rate of intake and assessment completion reported previously. Gains in treatment initiation and completion were negligible, however. Of the clients referred for services through Project SAFE, only 41% attended any treatment, and only 19% of the clients referred for substance abuse services completed treatment. Essentially, the results of drug-testing hair analyses were used in court to justify children's removal; they did not lead to any enhancement in service delivery.

The most extensively researched approach for enhancing substance abuse treatment delivery to families involved in child welfare is family treatment drug courts.[22] The first Family Treatment Drug Court was established in Reno, Nevada in 1994. The target population consisted of parents whose children were placed in the custody of protective services due to abuse or neglect related to substance abuse. As of June 2014, there were 303 Family Treatment Drug Courts nationwide. (http://www.ndcrc.org/content/how-many-drug-courts-are-there)

Characteristics of Family Treatment Drug Courts vary somewhat from court to court. In general, they include (1) substance abuse evaluation services available within the court building and frequently completed immediately following the initial child placement hearing; (2) regular, often weekly, court hearings to monitor parents' treatment compliance; (3) provision of substance abuse treatment and adjunctive wraparound services, often in the form of recovery coaches and other individualized services; (4) frequent drug testing; and (5) rewards, sanctions, and intensity of judicial surveillance linked to service compliance.

As reviewed elsewhere,[22] Family Treatment Drug Courts are associated with faster and greater rates of substance abuse treatment initiation, longer duration of treatment, and greater likelihood of treatment completion. Rates of treatment entry are between 80% and 90% for Family Treatment Drug Court cases, and approximately two-thirds of parents complete treatment.

Family Treatment Drug Courts also have been associated with fewer days in out-of-home placement for children and higher rates of family reunification, although rates of re-entry into care are high. In one study, days in out-of-home care were significantly fewer for children whose parents participated in Family Treatment Drug Courts, 403 versus 495 days, and also lower in a second study that examined this outcome, 642 versus 993 days. Across available studies, rates of reunification range from 42% to 69% for Family Treatment Drug Court cases, but 23% of children reunified with their parents re-enter care within two years. After over a year in out-of-home care, almost one-quarter of all children whose parents participated in Family Treatment Drug Courts are finding themselves back in the system.

Given the long time in out-of-home care and high rates of re-entry into the system for children of parents involved with Family Treatment Drug Courts, there is a need for the identification of novel, more effective, intervention approaches for providing substance abuse treatment to parents involved with child welfare. There is exciting preliminary data to support the efficacy of a home-based model of treatment called Building Stronger Families (BSF).[25,26] Building Stronger Families integrates two evidence-based treatment approaches: Multisystemic Therapy and Reinforcement-Based Treatment. Multisystemic Therapy is an empirically validated home- and community-based treatment for families of school-aged children with multiple complex mental health, material, and other service needs, and Reinforcement-Based Treatment is an empirically validated incentive-based intervention for adults with addictive disorders (e.g., earn a gift card if you have a clean urine test).

Building Stronger Families clinicians provide substance abuse, mental health, parenting, case management, and other services as needed, with 24/7 on-call services available to address crises that emerge after hours. Given the intensity of the intervention, these clinicians carry only four to six cases at a time, with treatment lasting about six months. The goals of the Building Stronger Families program are to eliminate parental substance misuse, address factors associated with child maltreatment, and keep children living with their families (parents or relatives) whenever possible. Family safety plans are developed with protective service workers and the treatment team, ideally with collaboration from members of the family's social network (e.g., friends, grandparents). Breathalyzer and urine drug testing is conducted randomly in the home a minimum of three times per week for the duration of treatment. Within the Building Stronger Families model, there is an understanding that relapse is a part of the recovery process. Decisions to remove children from their parents' homes are not based on the results of any particular drug test, but rather on parents' adherence to safety plans and their willingness to engage in substance abuse treatment.

In an initial feasibility study of the Building Stronger Families program with 54 families, 87% of the parents referred for treatment initiated services,

93% of those who began treatment services completed the program, and 75% of the parents retained custody of their children throughout the duration of treatment.[26] In a second quasi-experimental design study with 25 parents who received the Building Stronger Families intervention,[25] at posttreatment mothers showed significant reductions in alcohol use, drug use, and depressive symptoms, and their children reported significantly fewer anxiety symptoms. In addition, relative to 25 families who received standard community interventions, mothers who received Building Stronger Families were three times less likely to have another substantiated incident of maltreatment over a follow-up period of 24 months postreferral. Children of families who received Building Strong Families services also spent significantly fewer days in out-of-home placements than did their control counterparts. A more rigorous randomized study of Building Stronger Families treatment effectiveness is currently underway.

Programs such as Building Stronger Families are ideal for women like Maria, with intense mental health, substance abuse, and concrete service needs. With limited cell phone minutes, and no car to drive to appointments, there is something very powerful about creating a home-delivered, one-stop shopping service.

Addiction treatment, however, is an evolving area of multidisciplinary research and clinical care. There is now a medical specialty, addictions medicine,[27] and multiple drugs have been approved by the Food and Drug Administration (FDA) for the treatment of addictive disorders, with all of these medications found to be most efficacious when used in combination with counseling and self-help support interventions.[28] Vaccines against drug abuse that create antibodies that block the pharmacological effects of drugs are also currently under development,[29] with additional novel therapeutics on the horizon given emerging research on the effects of drug use on gene regulation in key brain regions implicated in sustaining addictive behaviors.[30]

There is often inadequate appreciation of addiction as a disease. As you will see as the story progresses, throughout the children's time in care they are repeatedly told, "Your mother has things she has to do to show she wants you and Sylar to come home. She's not doing them." If a parent were incapacitated by cancer, would we ever describe her inability to care for her children in this way? The take-home message in the statement repeatedly made by the children's worker is, "Your mother doesn't want you to come home; she doesn't really love you. If she did, she'd give up her drugs." Better to say, "Your mother is really sick, and she can't care for you now. Addiction is a very difficult disease to treat."

We and others are involved in ongoing research to understand the mechanisms by which early adversity confers risk for substance abuse later in life, and to understand how substance use in vulnerable individuals leads to changes in brain function that perpetuate addictive behaviors. To date, state-of-the art biomedical intervention approaches for the treatment of addiction disorders has not been integrated with novel in-home service delivery models to enhance recovery and sobriety outcomes in child welfare populations, and little is known about how to personalize treatments to optimize clinical outcomes. Suffice it to say, there is much work yet to be done, but many promising advances in the field. Unfortunately, the state-of-the art clinical care at the time Maria went through the system left 87% of the parents falling through the cracks.

4

After the Children's First Placement

(2 DAYS IN OUT-OF-HOME CARE)

It is two days since Sylar and Samya were taken from the shelter in the middle of the night. They are sitting around a dining room table at a Safe Home with Randy. Safe Homes were short-term group homes established for children at the time of initial placement with the goal of consolidating resources for assessment and treatment planning, and improving outcomes for children and families involved with the child welfare system. It turns out these programs cost the State on average an extra $10,000 per child with very little bang for the buck,[31] but we will discuss more about this experiment and group care within the child welfare system at a later time.

The Safe Home the children are in is a small single-story, wood-shingled ranch home located in a modest tree-lined residential neighborhood. While Randy and the children meet, the house is buzzing as most of the other children at the Safe Home are returning from school.

"I am sorry you guys missed school these past two days. I wasn't able to arrange the transportation to get you there."

"No worries," Samya said smiling. "We got to chill around the house and go shopping yesterday. I got three new outfits for school."

"Cool. You can show them to me when we pack up your stuff. I am here to take you back to your mom."

Samya springs out of her chair and gives Randy a hug.

Sylar's face does not exude the same enthusiasm. Before Randy arrived he was getting ready to go fishing with one of the Safe Home staff and a few of the other kids. He is disappointed about not getting to go on the outing, but accepts the change in plans with little protest. After discussing the aborted fishing plans he asks, "Where is our mom?"

"Your mom is staying in an apartment with her boyfriend Joseph."

Sylar and Samya turn and look at one another. Sylar and Samya had seen Joseph, the guy with the waist-length dreadlocks at the soup kitchen two or three times before, but they really do not know him.

Randy and the children get up from the table and not much else is said. Randy helps the children pack their clothes in black plastic garbage bags. The children then thank the Safe Home staff, and give them hugs before they walk out of the house to the blue State car in the driveway.

Joseph lives in the same town where the battered women's shelter is located, so Sylar and Samya will be able to continue in their same schools, but they do not know this on their ride to his house. It is only about a half-hour drive from the Safe Home to Joseph's house, but both children sleep most of the car ride there. They had not slept much in the past three days, and when they get in the car, a deep exhaustion overtakes them.

When Randy and the children pull up to the house, Maria and Joseph come outside to greet them. Samya springs from the car down the driveway and embraces her mother. She and her mother hold on to one another for a long time, rocking as they hold each other tight, oblivious to the chill in the late March air.

Sylar walks slowly down the hill, noting in his head that this is his eighth move in less than a year. He takes a deep breath and surveys his surroundings. The trees in the yard are still bare. The house is light mustard yellow; the paint is chipping and the porches on the ground level and second floor are each missing several posts. Sylar doubts they will be here for long, but when his mother hugs him, he allows himself to get swept up in the optimism of the moment. He relaxes and smiles, and reassures his mother as he wipes a stray tear off her cheek.

They all then go around the back of the house and climb the rickety steps to the second floor apartment. They sit down in the living room, Sylar in the stuffed chair across from the couch with his mother and sister. Randy has his mother sign some papers.

While Randy speaks, Sylar looks about the room. The living room is cluttered with a couch, coffee table, two stuffed chairs, a small dining table with four chairs, a TV, and a piano. Sylar is tempted to get up and look through the cassettes on the bookcase against the wall, but he knows it is not time to get up. He hears Randy say something about Joseph's father, who also lives in the home. He and Samya are not to be left alone with him. Although it has been more than a decade since Joseph's father has been arrested, he has over 50 arrests, including an arrest for sexual assault four charges that were nolled. Sylar does not know what sexual assault four charges are, but he figures it is not good. He gets an ache in the pit of his stomach as Randy talks on.

Randy leaves shortly after all the papers are signed, and does not come back for another week. It is a bit before dinnertime when he next comes to the house, and everyone is home except Joseph's father. Randy meets with the children first. Samya and Sylar take him down the back staircase off the kitchen to the first-floor apartment where their room is located. Joseph's grandmother, who owns the house, lives in the downstairs apartment. She used to be a licensed foster care provider and allows the children to stay in her spare bedroom. The children's room has the basics—two single beds and one dresser.

When Randy asks them how they like living there, Sylar lets him know that one of his friends from school lives across the street, and Samya replies, "It is definitely better than being at the shelter."

Neither of the children tells Randy that Joseph is dealing drugs, and neither of them tells him that some of the people coming through the house are kind of sketchy.

Randy leaves the children downstairs and goes upstairs to meet with Maria and Joseph. Maria and Joseph sit side-by-side on the couch. Joseph rests his hand on Maria's thigh, and Randy thinks they look comfortable enough with one another. After briefly exchanging pleasantries, Randy gets to business.

"You had an appointment at Clear Way that you missed last week."

It is evident by the tone in his voice that he is not happy that Maria missed her substance abuse treatment intake appointment. Maria tries to sound upbeat to lighten the mood.

"I know, but I've rescheduled. I have another appointment in two weeks."

"If you don't go, you increase the likelihood of the Department taking the children into custody again."

Maria looks straight into Randy's eyes, nods her head, and makes clear she understands what he is saying.

"I'll remind her," Joseph chimes in.

Randy then lets Maria know, "Your case is being substantiated for neglect and transferred to a new worker. I believe the woman who will be picking up your case is named Danielle. She'll be in touch shortly, but call me if you need anything before then."

Investigation workers are only involved with families through the forensic evaluation. Once substantiated, cases are transferred to new workers for ongoing case supervision. Maria thanks Randy for his help, and assures him that she will do what she needs to do.

Two weeks later, the day after Maria's scheduled substance abuse treatment intake appointment at Clear Way, there is a knock on the back door in the late afternoon. The stereo is blaring and at first Maria does not hear the knock.

When Maria opens the door she sees a dark-haired pregnant woman in a suit with a folder in her hand. She assumes it is her new worker, Danielle (DCF-W4). Maria smiles and invites her in, then turns her head toward Joseph and signals for him to turn off the stereo. When Danielle walks into the apartment, her foot falls through a hole covered by a mat just inside the doorway.

Danielle notices the children sitting in the corner of the room and asks Maria if she can speak with them first. She then walks back to the dining room table where Sylar and Samya are sitting. Samya is eating chocolate pudding, and Sylar is working on some homework. Danielle asks them both about school, but only Samya answers her questions. Sylar keeps his focus on his work, only looking up at her once or twice. He lets his sister do the talking for the two of them.

Sylar and Samya then go down the back staircase to their room. Maria, Joseph, and Danielle sit around the cramped dining room table. Maria feels tense and her leg bounces nervously. Danielle lets Maria know she is pleased to be working with her, wants to get to know her, but makes it clear that she has some concerns.

"You missed your appointment at Clear Way yesterday."

"It was yesterday?" Maria looks genuinely surprised when she asks this question. Her leg continues to bounce.

"You need to call and reschedule your intake appointment. We also need you to take a urine drug test, and you don't need an appointment for that. You should be able to stop there any time for a urine tox screen."

"I'll go later today. We don't have a car so I have to walk everywhere, but I'll go later today."

"It will probably be too late to go today, but you can go tomorrow any time after nine o'clock."

Maria tells Danielle that she needs to find a psychiatrist in the area. She takes trazodone, Prozac, Seroquel, and clonidine for her PTSD and depression, and has run out of her clonidine. "I've started to hear voices. I think it's because I've run out of the clonidine."

"Are the voices telling you to do anything?"

"No, they're just like whispers, but they make me afraid someone is in the house." There's a vacant look to Maria's expression. She looks fragile and Danielle is unnerved listening to her talk about the voices.

While they are talking at the dining room table, Joseph's grandmother comes up the back staircase through the kitchen and into the living room. She does not seem to notice Danielle who has her back to the kitchen door.

"The check you dropped off is only for $400. Where's the rest of the money you owe me for rent?"

An argument ensues; Joseph's grandmother screams that she is owed $300 more, and Maria barks back that she paid her the amount to which they agreed. In-between curses and the slamming of doors, Danielle is able to ascertain that there is no written lease.

After Joseph's grandmother goes back downstairs, Danielle suggests Maria think about finding another apartment. Although Danielle was able to appease Joseph's grandmother in the short-run, it is apparent Joseph's grandmother only backed down to avoid further confrontation with Danielle in the house.

The next day, after Sylar and Samya leave for school, Maria gets ready to go to Clear Way. She puts on jeans, a nice top, and mascara. It is a cool morning as she leaves the house, with the promise of spring in the air. As Maria walks down her street she looks at the budding flowers on several of the trees and the daffodils abloom on the side of the road. She also wonders about Sylar's missing SSI check. She is worried about money for groceries and is not sure whom she should call to track down the check. She does not have a lot of minutes left on her cell phone and she hates calling State agencies. They can leave a person on hold forever. The tension in her shoulders and on the top of her back makes her want to get high. She flashes back to returning to the shelter and being told by the director that her kids were in care and the thought of getting high disappears. She stretches her neck from side to side and keeps walking. The whiz of the cars as she walks under the overpass freaks her out. She looks at the garbage strewn on the railway tracks on the side of the road, and then concentrates on finding the Court building, because it is located on the same street as Clear Way, and marks where she will need to turn.

When Maria arrives at Clear Way, she walks through the glass doors, past the empty vinyl chairs in the waiting room, and signs in with the receptionist. No hair analysis this time. She just has to pee in a cup. She will not be meeting to talk with anyone for a couple of weeks. She completes a release form and gives it back to the receptionist, takes the plastic cup she is given in exchange, and walks with an escort down the hall to one of the empty exam rooms. There is a bathroom located inside the exam room. Maria is instructed to leave the door open while she pees. Maria tries not to think about the person in the doorway staring at her. She does her business, hands the woman the cup, washes her hands, and walks out of the exam room and out the clinic without saying anything to anybody. The three-quarter mile walk home then passes in a blur.

The following day while sitting in her cubby, Danielle gets a call from Clear Way with the results of Maria's urine toxicology screen. It is negative, indicating no recent drug use. Danielle smiles as she hangs up the phone, then logs onto the computer and begins typing a note in Maria's electronic chart. While she is typing, the telephone rings again. It is the social worker from Sylar's school.

"I am calling to let you know that Sylar is out from school again today. This makes 17 missed days of school in the past month and a half."

"Have you spoken with his mother?"

"I haven't been able to get her on the phone. There was an educational planning meeting scheduled for Sylar last week, but she didn't show up. We need releases signed to get his old school records from New York."

"How is Sylar when he's at school?"

"He's a sweet kid. He isn't any trouble in class, but when I've met with him, he's gotten teary eyed. He seems depressed to me."

Danielle suggests the social worker call the child abuse hotline and file a neglect report. She then calls Samya's school to see how she is doing. Samya's school guidance counselor says Samya never misses school. She describes Samya as "sweet" and "confident" and says she has no concerns.

Scott (DCF-W5) is assigned to investigate the educational neglect charges filed by Sylar's school social worker. He runs background checks before going out to the house and uncovers a report previously missed. Joseph was arrested on domestic violence charges four months earlier in an incident with a former girlfriend.

Scott meets with Joseph and Maria together the first time he comes to the house. Joseph says he is court-mandated to go to domestic violence classes and that he has attended two classes thus far. He says he finds them helpful. Maria says Sylar is choosing not to go to school and purposely missing the bus. She says she has no car to take him when he misses the bus, and currently has no minutes on her phone to call the school and report him out.

Maria then asks to speak with Scott in private on the back porch. Tears form in her eyes as she speaks.

"I know I gotta find a better place to live. My kids need a home."

She talks about knowing how hard the past year was on both of them—Sylar in particular. She talks about being stressed because Joseph's grandmother keeps raising the rent and threatening to call the police and kick them out, and being worried about money because Sylar's SSI check is missing. She also talks about Joseph's dad creeping her out; making sexual advances toward her. Then after hesitating, she adds, "And on top of all this—I'm pregnant. What was I thinking getting involved with a guy so young and immature? I must have been pretty needy."

Scott is reassuring. He lets Maria know the Department referred her to the parent aide program. This will provide her with someone who can help her find housing, track down Sylar's missing social security check, and deal with all the stuff on her plate. He lets her know that she needs to confirm the appointment with the parent aide, or the aide will not come out to the house. Maria says she will get to a phone the next day to confirm the appointment.

Scott then goes back in the house and down the back stairway off the kitchen to get Sylar from his bedroom. They go for a walk down the street to talk. Sylar promises to go to school the next day and to try to make it every day until the end of the school year. Sylar says he is angry, however. He is sick of all the moves, and worried they will be back in a shelter again. He also says he had been missing school because his family situation makes him feel like he just does not care—and because he is worried about his mom.

Scott did not ask what Sylar means, but the phrase, "worried about my mom," struck him.

The next day after Sylar and Samya both go to school, Maria takes off for the DCF office to make some telephone calls. It is another nice spring day. As she walks by the post office and sees all the mail trucks she starts thinking about the missing SSI check. She wonders if Joseph's grandmother stole it.

When she gets to the DCF office, there are no phones immediately available. Within a few minutes the receptionist buzzes her around back, then shows her to an empty cubby where she can make some calls. She confirms her appointment with the parent aide for the next day. The woman sounds nice. She also speaks to someone from the social security benefits office. They are going to put a stop on the other check, reissue the payment, and send it to her new address. Maria hopes she will still be at the address by the time the check arrives.

Before she leaves the office she runs into Danielle. She lets her know that she is pregnant but thinking about having an abortion.

"Joseph don't want me to have no abortion though. I'm not sure what he'll do if I get one."

On the half-mile walk home Maria tries to imagine having another baby. It is the last thing she needs. Joseph is the last thing she needs right now, but he gave her a roof over her head, and that is what she needed to get the kids back.

Two days later Maria goes back to the DCF office to use the phone again. No phone is available, but she has a chance to speak with Danielle again.

"Where were you yesterday? You missed your intake appointment at Clear Way."

"Joseph had a seizure. I couldn't leave him. Mrs. W. the parent aide was at the house when it happened. She can vouch for me."

"You'll need to call to reschedule. You can come back later in the day to use the phones."

Maria leaves the DCF office, but she never makes it back that afternoon to call and reschedule her Clear Way appointment. Maria is worried and stressed; and that is the same state she is in when she comes back a week later for an appointment with Danielle. Nothing is fixed. She is still pregnant. Joseph's dad is still hitting on her, and Joseph's grandmother is still threatening to put them out on the streets.

Things continue to get worse over the following week. The next time Maria comes back to the DCF office she is with Sylar, and the first thing Danielle notices is Maria's eye is bruised and her face is swollen. Sylar lets Danielle know that Joseph beat on his mom and she had to go to the hospital the night before. His mom had a concussion. Danielle asks Sylar to stay in the waiting room, and she takes Maria into a family visit room so they can talk in private.

"What happened?"

Maria minimizes the domestic violence, and it is clear to Danielle that Maria does not want to talk about it. Danielle feels sick as she looks at Maria's bruised eye and swollen face. *How could she talk on like it is no big deal? And isn't Joseph in the midst of some court mandated domestic violence treatment?*

Danielle decides to change the subject. "Have you been able to get started in counseling yet?"

"What's the point? I'd leave the session and be back in the same old stressful situation."

"Did you get your medications refilled?"

"Not yet. I'm just so stressed out I feel like killing everybody."

"What about going up to the hospital for an evaluation? Maybe an inpatient stay? You can get back on your meds and get a break from everything."

"And what about my kids?"

Danielle tries to persuade Maria to consider going inpatient for treatment—or at least to the ER for a psychiatric evaluation, but it is pointless. Danielle feels frustrated. What is she supposed to do if Maria does not follow through with any of the services DCF found for her? Danielle is at a loss.

Danielle asks if she can speak with Sylar alone. Maria goes out to the waiting room, and Sylar and Danielle go into the family visit room. They sit side by side on the couch. Danielle asks Sylar why he is out from school.

"We didn't get home from the hospital until really late. My mom let me sleep in."

Danielle asks Sylar how he is doing. Sylar has not showered and he looks like he is still wearing his clothes from the previous day.

Sylar talks about how tired he is. He does not like living with Joseph and Joseph's grandmother, and he is sick of moving. He is also tired of worrying and looking out for his mother.

"I need a vacation."

Sylar then goes on to talk about wanting to go back to the Safe Home. He confesses that he never really wanted to leave the Safe Home.

There is a treatment planning conference scheduled for later in the day. Danielle lets Maria know to come back. Danielle plans to talk with her supervisor, update her, and together make a plan for next steps. Things are deteriorating rapidly, and Sylar needs *a vacation*.

A few hours later Maria shows up for the treatment planning conference at the DCF office with Sylar. Samya is not yet home from school. They check in with the receptionist and are told to have a seat in the waiting room.

Maria and Sylar sit down in the vinyl chairs close to the television set. Maria's thighs stick to the chair. She distracts herself from her worries by focusing on the soap opera playing on the TV, and bouncing her leg repeatedly to dispense wound up extra energy. Sylar closes his eyes, stretches his legs out long in front of him, and lets his head fall back.

After a few minutes, Danielle comes over and greets them. She asks Sylar to stay in the waiting room and escorts Maria to the conference room down the hall. When they arrive in the room, there are two other women sitting at the rectangular conference table. Maria has never seen them before. When Danielle closes the door, Maria feels like she will suffocate. There are no windows in the room, and although she can tell there is air conditioning, the air feels stifling. She sits in a seat on the opposite side of the table across from the three women.

A woman who appears to be Danielle's supervisor runs the meeting. The woman begins by summarizing the case history.

"Mother had been in a shelter where she was receiving intensive mental health services. Mother has a history of substance abuse. Mother relocated and is living with an abusive boyfriend. Since moving, mother has not followed through with the recommended services."

Throughout the meeting, the supervisor speak as though Maria were not in the room, continually referring to her as "the mother." The three women exchange glances among themselves, but avoid Maria's gaze. Maria tries to interject and explain why she has yet to begin substance abuse treatment or reinitiate mental health services. She also tries to minimize the severity of the ongoing domestic violence, but the swelling around her eye makes her words unconvincing. After being shot down for the third or fourth time, Maria has the sense she is on trial and the verdict has already been cast.

She then hears the words she feared most, "We are going to take the children into custody again today."

Tears erupt and she jumps up from her chair.

"You take those kids from me and I got nothin' to live for."

There are shouts and more tears, and then a wave of resignation comes over Maria. The weight in her chest pulls her back down into her seat. As she looks around the room, it is as if the mute button has been pressed. The supervisor's mouth is moving, but Maria hears nothing until the buzzer from the intercom breaks through her numbness.

Through the intercom the security guard announces the arrival of the case aide who had been sent to pick up Samya from school. Maria's eyes shoot to the intercom on the wall. Before she can say anything, Danielle goes out to the waiting room to greet Samya and bring her and Sylar back to the conference room.

When the children walk into the room Maria blurts out, "They are taking you again."

Samya bursts into tears. Sylar hangs back near the doorway. Maria goes up to Samya and hugs her. She strokes her hair and looks into Samya's eyes and says, "Baby you won't be gone long. I'm gonna do what I gotta do so you can come home."

Samya looks up at her mother. Maria reaches out to Sylar and pulls both children up against her. Maria then tries to be reassuring and says with a slight smile, "Maybe the time will be good for us—a time to get our heads on straight."

After a bit Danielle suggests Maria head home, but asks her to come back the following day so she can get health history and other information about the kids. The other two women who had been in the room for the conference left at some earlier point, but Maria did not notice them leave.

The children are then brought to the room in the DCF office where they had stayed the first time they were taken into custody. They recognize the TV, VCR, and the two couches with the wooden armrests that made it impossible to sleep that night. Danielle brings the kids some snacks. She lets them know they will be going to a different Safe Home this time. Sylar and Samya play Uno, watch cartoons, and eat their snacks while they wait for all the arrangements to be finalized. They do not talk about what just happened at the meeting or what is coming next. To someone looking into the room from the outside, there is nothing remarkable about the scene—just two kids playing, seemingly having a good time.

Domestic Violence and Child Welfare

Domestic violence impacts millions of families worldwide.[32] In the United States alone, lifetime prevalence studies suggest between 20% and 30% of women will be assaulted by an intimate partner, and between 5% and 20% of children will witness a parent being abused.[33] Domestic violence is especially prevalent within child welfare samples, with approximately 35% of all child protective service cases reporting a lifetime history of domestic violence.[34] Among cohorts of maltreated children who have entered out-of-home care, approximately 70% have witnessed severe domestic violence, with rates approaching 90% among the subset of children whose parents also struggle with substance abuse problems.[35]

Results of three recent reviews of court-mandated batterer interventions concluded that the programs are of negligible benefit at reducing partner violence.[36-38] At the time Samya and Sylar were placed into care, Joseph was participating in a court-ordered domestic violence treatment referred to as the Duluth Model, which focuses on education about power and control.[39] According to this model, the primary cause of domestic violence is patriarchal ideology and societal sanctioning of men's power and control over women. The fundamental tool of the Duluth model is the "Power and Control Wheel." It is used to illustrate how men use intimidation, male privilege, isolation, money, emotional abuse, and violence to control women. The goal of the intervention is to make the batterer aware of the experience of women who have been abused and to help abusive men become more self-reflective with regard to their behavior. It is implemented in a variety of protocols ranging from 8 to 36 weeks, and is the unchallenged treatment of choice in many communities. There is, however, little evidence of its effectiveness.[38]

Another common approach to batterer treatment is Group Cognitive Behavioral Treatment (CBT), in which learning nonviolence is the primary focus. The CBT therapist works to point out the pros and cons of violence along with providing skills training (e.g., anger management, communication skills, assertiveness, relaxation training) to promote alternatives to violence. Available research, however, also suggests that CBT interventions have no significant impact on re-abuse rates among batterers.[38]

Mandatory arrest is another strategy used in many communities in cases of domestic violence. It was hypothesized that criminal justice ramifications would deter perpetrators from continuing to use violence. Results of a large scale ($N = 4032$), multisite study of mandatory arrest for domestic violence, however, also failed to demonstrate a benefit of mandatory arrest on perpetrator violence.[38]

What about interventions focused on victims? Evaluated interventions intended for victims of domestic violence have been based in (1) shelters, (2) prenatal clinics, or (3) the community, using police–social service outreach and advocacy. Studies of these victim-focused interventions, however, report recidivism rates comparable to, or greater than, those reported in perpetrator focused studies.[38]

Are there any promising approaches for reducing domestic violence? The best available preliminary data come from models that address the co-occurring problems frequently experienced by batterers. The co-occurrence of substance abuse problems among batterers is high, with estimates ranging from 40% to 92% across studies.[38] There is emerging evidence to suggest that recidivism rates are lower when batterers are provided treatments that address substance abuse and partner violence simultaneously in integrated programs.[40-44] To the best of my knowledge, only one study has combined behavioral interventions for alcohol treatment and anger management with a pharmacological intervention.[45] This study enrolled male alcoholics who had two or more incidents of domestic violence within the past year. All men were provided standard cognitive and motivational therapies, together with self-help groups (e.g., Alcoholics Anonymous) to address their alcoholism, plus CBT interventions to address their violent behaviors. Half the men were randomized to receive fluoxetine (e.g., Prozac), given the role of serotonin in aggressive behavior, and the other half were given the combined behavioral interventions addressing their alcohol and anger problems plus placebo, a sugar pill. Fluoxetine plus the integrated behavior therapies was associated with lower perpetrator ratings of irritability, and fewer episodes of domestic violence reported by the spouses.

Although these results are promising, there are very few places where integrated treatment interventions such as these are available. Typically a father with these co-occurring problems who is involved with the child welfare system will be mandated to substance abuse counseling, anger management, and parenting classes, which almost always involves trying to coordinate treatment from three different agencies.

Recently Lam and colleagues augmented Behavioral Couples Therapy with Parent Management Training to address these co-occurring issues. Behavioral Couples Therapy is an integrated treatment that was found to be more effective than individual substance abuse treatment alone in reducing recidivism for men suffering from comorbid substance abuse and domestic violence.[41] In Behavioral Couples Therapy, males receive weekly individual and group drug abuse counseling, both of which emphasize cognitive-behavioral anger management and coping skills training. Additionally, males and their female partners meet conjointly for weekly sessions. The joint sessions are used to

(a) help male partners remain abstinent; (b) teach more effective communication skills; and (c) increase positive behavioral exchanges between partners.

In the combined Parenting Skills Behavioral Couples Therapy intervention, treatment is 12-weeks with 6-weeks dedicated to parent skills training.[42,43] Like Behavioral Couples Therapy, the combined treatment was associated with significant improvement in substance abuse and partner violence, but additionally, with improvement in parenting behaviors, reduced rates of referral to protective services, and marked improvement on multiple indices of child adjustment. Couples therapy approaches, however, are only appropriate in mild-to-moderate family aggression and are not recommended in cases of severe family violence.

Although there are promising preliminary data to support integrative treatment models that address domestic violence, substance abuse, and parenting issues, as noted previously, such programs are not readily available. In addition, further research is required to establish their efficacy with diverse populations. There are several other innovative intervention strategies on the horizon.[44,46] Although controlled studies of many of these new approaches have not yet been published in the scientific literature, descriptions of the programs and preliminary outcome data can be found on the website for the National Resource Center on Domestic Violence.[46] (See Reference 38 for a review of this topic; and see Reference 46 for the website of the National Resource Center on Domestic Violence, which includes links for relevant resources, training, technical assistance, and information about promising new intervention programs.)

Like work in the area of substance abuse, the prediction and treatment of violent behavior is also an evolving area of research and clinical care. Insights on the neural systems that mediate aggressive behavior, and advances in pharmacological approaches to enhance the effectiveness of behavioral interventions to treat problematic aggressive behavior are active areas of investigation.[47] Integration of this work with child welfare practice, however, is in its infancy.

At the time Maria went through the system, only standard perpetrator and victim domestic violence programs were available, and over the years the children were in the system, Maria continued to cycle through a series of violent relationships. But let's not get ahead in the narrative; let's return to the family's story and see what happened after the children are taken into custody a second time.

5

The Children's Second Placement

(3 DAYS IN OUT-OF-HOME CARE)

The smell of burnt coffee hangs in the air. Danielle's cubby is crowded with stacks of paper. She stares at the computer screen with Maria's electronic file open in front of her, typing up notes from the meeting the afternoon before. Her train of thought is broken when the phone rings.

"DCF—Can I help you?"

It is Mrs. W., the parent aide who works with Maria. Danielle tells Mrs. W. about the children's placement, and the two speak about the Department's goals for Maria. Before Mrs. W. gets off the phone she tells Danielle about her last encounter with Sylar.

"I took him out to lunch yesterday; wanted to give him a chance to talk about the night before when he went to the hospital with his mother. He told me something happened to him that he never told anyone, but he didn't elaborate."

"Did you ask him what it was?"

"No. He got quiet and I didn't want to push."

"Oh, OK."

When the call ends Danielle resumes typing on her keyboard. She finishes the note she had been writing in the electronic record before the phone rang, and then she documents her call with Mrs. W. The note ends with information about Sylar's lunch with Mrs. W. "Sylar told Mrs. W. that he needed to get away. He also told Mrs. W. that something happened that he never told anyone, but he did not elaborate."

Danielle never follows up with Sylar about this, and Sylar never sees Mrs. W. again.

Maria arrives at the DCF office for her appointment at about the same time Danielle finishes her notes on the computer. Joseph is with her. Maria's heart races as she opens the heavy glass door and walks toward the receptionist to announce her arrival. She is told to wait. Maria sits upright in her chair and tries to focus on the show playing on the television set in the waiting room.

After a few minutes Danielle comes out to greet Maria. As soon as Maria notices her, she asks, "When can I see my kids?"

"I'll let you know. I'll take care of scheduling a visit in the next week or so."

As Danielle replies, a wave of disgust hits her. She looks at Joseph, and then at Maria's bruised and swollen face. She then asks, "Would you like to meet in private?"

"No, I don't mind if Joseph joins us."

With the children gone, all thoughts Maria had of leaving Joseph evaporated. She could not tolerate being alone, especially now. The three walk single file down the hall to the conference room. As they pass a mirror, Maria stares at the eyes of the stranger looking back at her. She does not recognize her own reflection.

Once in the conference room, Danielle sits on one side of the table and Maria and Joseph sit side by side across from her. Images of the meeting the day before flash in front of Maria's eyes. Joseph gently rests his hand on Maria's lower arm and it soothes her. The reality of where she is and what happened sinks in. During the meeting Maria can hear herself talk, but it feels as though the words are coming from someone else. The necessary information is exchanged, and in a haze Maria again leaves the DCF office without Sylar and Samya.

On the walk home, everything Danielle said swirls around in her head. *The children will not be coming home in two days like the last time they were taken into custody. It is up to you how long the children remain in care. In order for the children to come home, you have to be actively involved in mental health treatment, drug-free, in stable housing, and out of all violent relationships. You will have visits every other week with the children. You also can come to the DCF office up to twice a week for supervised calls to the children.* Maria mulls over with disbelief the thought of supervised calls to her own children.

The children are several towns away at a Safe Home. It is a different Safe Home than the one they went to last time. Instead of being located in a small house in a residential area, this Safe Home is part of a large multiprogram treatment center. The colonial red brick buildings with white trim, the rolling green lawns, and the huge maple trees make it look more like a private New England prep school than a shelter and residential treatment program for kids. The Safe Home is situated in a small white cottage behind the main quadrangle and it houses up to 13 children. There is even an outdoor swimming pool on campus, along with a huge indoor gymnasium. Sylar thinks it is a great place for a vacation, better than he imagined.

Almost two weeks pass before the children are scheduled for a visit with their mother. A DCF case aide drives Maria and Joseph the 30 minutes from their home to the center. The visit takes place in the visitation room, a small conference room in the Administration Building on the far side of campus from where the Safe Home is located. Maria had asked the aide to stop at McDonald's on their way, and she sets up lunch on the table before the kids arrive in the visitation room. Sylar and Samya are escorted to the visit across the sprawling lawns by a cottage staff member. They walk there in silence, the warm spring sun beating down on them, lost in their own thoughts.

When they enter the Administration Building, their senses are inundated with the smell of McDonald's French fries. As the door to the visitation room opens, screams of joy emit from the room. The four hug enthusiastically, and if Sylar had any hesitations, they are not apparent. To the staff, Joseph looks like an integral and well-loved member of the family. The children are skilled at adapting to various circumstances, and they can hide their true feelings when necessary.

Maria lets the children know she has an intake for therapy scheduled for the following day, and an appointment for a substance abuse evaluation the day after that. She lets the children know she is working with Mrs. W. to find an apartment, and trying to get into a program that provides subsidized housing and addiction and mental health services.

"I'm doin' what I gotta do."

She is confident and animated as she speaks.

She then adds while passing out the Happy Meals to the kids, "This will probably be our last visit. You should be home before. . ."

The staff member interrupts her and interjects in a somewhat harsh tone, "Nothing is set about the children coming home."

These sobering words, however, do not extinguish the excitement in the room. Maria really believes the children will be coming home soon, and the children believe her, too. Sylar thinks to himself, *Maybe this time things will be different.*

Sylar and Samya spend the remainder of the visit telling Maria and Joseph about the Safe Home and the new school they just started, their sixth school this academic year. Staff records note that both children were anxious about starting yet another school, but Samya "... appeared to blend easily into her new class making several new friends. There were no difficulties with assignments, and overall the nine-day school experience was positive." Sylar, too, "transitioned well...making new friends...proud of his academic success...showing cottage staff high grades he received on tests."

The children also talk about the swimming pool, outings for ice cream, and friends living in the cottage. Sylar talks a lot about a girl named Sabina that he is spending most of his time with. Samya teases him saying he has a crush on this girl.

There is also much the children do not speak about. Sylar does not talk about his conversation with the cottage social worker, in which he revealed he has been thinking about death since he was four years old. Samya also leaves unspoken her conversation with the social worker about the domestic violence between her mother and her mother's ex- back in New York. Samya reassures herself that nothing she said should jeopardize their chances of going home; she only spoke about the old stuff, not the recent stuff. Samya's sadness about being away from her mother is also not discussed, and she does not talk about how she feels worried all the time about her mother's safety.

The hour-long visit ends in a flash. They all hug again and part reluctantly. After the visit, a staff member brings Sylar to school; Samya goes back to the cottage. She does not feel well enough to go to school.

Two weeks later Samya celebrates her first birthday in care. The cottage staff serve a cake for her birthday after dinner that night, and she gets a small radio and CD player as a present. She smiles on the outside while all the kids sing, "Happy Birthday," ignoring the feeling in the pit of her stomach and the thoughts of her mother that cloud her mood.

A few days later she receives a telephone call from her mother. Maria had stopped by to see Danielle to complain that there had been no visit for Samya's birthday. Danielle is not in the office, but her supervisor is, and she arranges for Maria to call Samya. When they speak on the phone, Maria lets Samya know how sorry she is that she did not see her for her birthday, and she tells her how much she loves her. The supervisor lets them know a visit is scheduled for later in the week. After Samya hangs up the phone she thinks about how things get out of control sometimes with Joseph, and she hopes her mother is all right.

When Maria gets off the telephone, she lets Danielle's supervisor know that she is doing what she has to do. She has seen her therapist three times, met with the psychiatrist, started on medication, and completed the substance abuse evaluation. She is also working really hard to find housing. She and Mrs. W. found an apartment, but she needs help with the security deposit. She also said Joseph is doing what he is supposed to do. There have been no fights in a bit, and he is almost done with the domestic violence program he was court ordered to attend after the incident with his ex-girlfriend. The supervisor says she will pass along the information to Danielle.

Back at the cottage, Sylar and Sabina continue to grow closer, spending most of their spare time together. One night Sylar cannot fall asleep. He tosses and turns for hours. He decides to sneak out of his room and down to Sabina's room. He knocks on the door, but she does not reply. He pushes lightly at the door, and looks over his shoulder when it creeks. Sabina is sleeping on her single mattress, with her back to the door of the room, curled up in a fetal position. Sylar does not go under the covers, but he climbs on the bed and gently wraps his body around her. His cotton pajamas leave him feeling a bit cool. Sylar begins to rock his hips gently back and forth. The rhythmic movement soothes him. He becomes aroused, and then Sabina wakes up.

Sabina screams, jumps from the bed, and runs out of the room. Two night shift staff hear her screams and come running. Sabina is crying. She repeats again and again between heaving breaths, "He tried to hump me!" She refuses to look directly at Sylar as she speaks.

A few kids pop their heads out into the hallway. The staff orders everyone back to their beds. The female staff member on duty then takes Sabina downstairs to the kitchen. The male staff member takes Sylar into the director's office.

Sylar is confused. Sabina's screams reverberate in his head. The angry and disappointed looks of the staff stab him in his gut. There is a ringing in his ears, and he feels as if he is outside his body watching the events of the night unfold. Scenes of things that happened when he was living with his mother replay in his head. He closes his eyes hoping the images and the sensation that he is back in time will go away.

After a few minutes he looks up with dazed eyes and realizes the staff had been talking to him this whole time. He has not heard a word that was said. He tries to focus in on what the staff is saying. He realizes he is being asked why he had gone into Sabina's room. He says the first thing that comes to his mind, "I went to give her back a toy." The erection that still protrudes through his pajama pants, however, makes his explanation seem unlikely.

The staff brings him back to his room and stays stationed outside his door for the remainder of the night. The next day there are multiple meetings to discuss the incident. Sylar sticks with his return-the-toy story. He writes a letter of apology, but Sylar's friendship with Sabina is never the same.

At the time, someone probably asked him if anyone ever sexually abused him, but nothing is noted anywhere in the record.

The children's next visit with their mother a day later is a discharge planning meeting, which both Danielle and the cottage social worker attend. Maria again brought McDonald's lunches for the children, along with other gifts. At the meeting, Danielle reveals the Department's two-prong plan. The children will be discharged from the Safe Home at the end of the month, just shy of two months after they were admitted. If all the necessary elements are in place, they may be returned to Maria's care. If not, a referral was made for a foster care placement. Both Samya and Maria are furious at the mention of foster care. Sylar sits quietly and looks neither pleased nor distressed at the prospect.

The day after this meeting, Maria learns that her apartment fell through. Danielle then finalizes the referral for a foster care placement. A couple, whose children are grown and out of the home, is identified—the Olsens.

They are first-time foster parents, but Mrs. Olsen knows about foster care first hand. She had a foster sister, although her foster sister did not come to live with her family via any official channels. When Mrs. Olsen was in the seventh grade there was a girl in her class who came to school wearing the same outfit multiple days in a row. One day this girl came to school with a box with all her clothes in it. When Mrs. Olsen asked her why she had all her clothes with her, the girl told her she was leaving home. Mrs. Olsen could not understand. The only time she heard of kids leaving home was on television or in books like *The Adventures of Huckleberry Finn*. She then asked the girl why she was leaving home and the girl replied, "My father is messing with me." Mrs. Olsen did not know what that meant at the time, but she knew if it was enough to make you want to leave home, it had to be real bad. Mrs. Olsen told the girl she could come live with her. They rode the bus home together after school that day. When Mrs. Olsen's mother heard the girl's reason for leaving home, she let the girl stay. There were 10 children in the family. What was one more? The girl's parents never came to look for her. The police were never called. This girl grew up in Mrs. Olsen's home, and Mrs. Olsen and that girl consider each other sisters still, over 40 years later.

A few days after the discharge planning meeting with their mother, Danielle's supervisor comes to the Safe Home to introduce the children to the Olsens. The children had seen the supervisor on a few occasions, like at the meeting the day they came into care, but they had never really spoken with her before. Danielle's supervisor meets alone with Samya and Sylar in the director's office at the cottage. As she begins talking about the Olsens, Samya storms out of the office. She wants nothing to do with moving to a foster home. Sylar is curious and feeling ready to move on from the Safe Home; it has felt uncomfortable since the incident with Sabina.

The Olsens are waiting up in the Administration Building. With coaxing from one of the cottage staff, Samya agrees to walk across campus and meet them. She is scared—scared of meeting them, scared of liking them, and scared of never going home.

When they walk into the visitation room, the first thing Samya notices is that the table is bare. There are no McDonald's lunches, just the sterile conference table. The woman at the table is not her mother and that guy with her is definitely not Joseph. Mrs. Olsen is probably the same age as her grandmother, and looks a tad like her at quick glance. Mrs. Olsen is wearing a gray dress, and Mr. Olsen has on a navy blue suit with a flag pin in his lapel. They look like they both just came from church. Mr. Olsen also looks a little like Mr. Jefferson from the TV series *The Jeffersons* with the song, "Movin on Up," but as it turns out, he has a much sweeter disposition.

Samya sits in a chair away from the table. Through most of the visit she looks out the window and tries not to pay attention to the conversation in the room. When the Olsens speak to her, she does not look at them and replies with one-word answers.

Sylar sits in a seat right next to Mrs. Olsen. Sylar wants to learn as much as he can about these new potential foster parents. Do they have other children? Do their children live in their house with them? How many rooms are in their house? Will he have his own bedroom? Do they have toys? Do they watch Dragon Ball Z?

While Mrs. Olsen answers Sylar's many questions, Mr. Olsen goes and sits next to Samya. He lets her know she does not have to come live with them, but if she does, he is sure that Mrs. Olsen will treat her like a princess. He tells her Mrs. Olsen never had a daughter. He does not mention the baby girl they lost when she was only six weeks old. Samya listens as Mr. Olsen describes the various ways Mrs. Olsen would spoil her. She smiles briefly and looks up at him, uncertain how to take it all in. She then thinks to herself, it may be okay to stay with these people until her mom gets an apartment and she and Sylar can go home.

Racial Disparities in Child Welfare

After the incident with Sabina, Sylar was not referred for mental health counseling or a psychosexual evaluation; a specialized assessment to determine risk, understand the issues that led to his actions, and help develop a treatment plan to address inappropriate sexualized behaviors. The incident with Sabina was not the only red flag during his stay at the Safe Home; Sylar also reported thoughts of death since the age of four. His conversation with the parent aide right before he was placed also suggested a need for services; *something happened that he never told anyone.*

What if Sylar were white instead of a moderately dark-skinned biracial male? Statistically, he would have been more likely to be referred for mental health counseling. Multiple studies have shown that African American children within the child welfare system are less likely to receive mental health services.[48-50] Sylar does eventually receive a specialized psychosexual evaluation and mental health services, but access to them is quite delayed, and as you will see as the story unfolds, this had significant costs.

The child welfare system is plagued with multiple levels of racial disparities. Although African American and white women are equally likely to test positive for drugs at the birth of a child, African American women are more likely to be reported to child protective services as a result.[51] Once reported to child welfare, after controlling for poverty and other risk factors, African American women are less likely to be referred for differential response family assessment interventions and more likely to be assigned the forensic intervention track.[52]

Nationwide, African American children are almost twice as likely as white children to be victims in verified reports of child abuse and neglect,[53] and more likely to be in foster care placement than receive in-home services, even when they have the same family problems and characteristics as white children.[54] The problem of racial disparities is particularly profound in some jurisdictions; for example, in New York City, mixed race and minority youth comprise approximately 90% of all children in foster care.[55]

There is some evidence that racial disparities are fueled in part by poverty and its associated risks,[56] but the data cited above suggest this is not the whole picture. The issue of racial disparities in the child welfare system is at the forefront of reform efforts; entire journal volumes have been devoted to this topic,[57] and The Annie E. Casey Foundation has a working group on racial disproportionality that compiled a monograph of promising practices to address racial disproportionality in child welfare.[58] (See Reference 58 for website to download report.)

Concerns about racial disparities also sparked the moratorium on our research. Because minorities are overrepresented in the foster care system, some administrators worried that our genetics research would stigmatize minorities. The National Institutes of Health, however, prioritizes research with minorities, because research with Caucasian populations does not generalize to all ethnic minorities. There are real race differences in susceptibility to some diseases; for example, I am Jewish and my children were screened for Tay-Sachs disease in utero. There are also race differences in response to medication for diseases like heart failure, prompting many to advocate for including African Americans and other population subgroups in clinical trials to devise optimal treatment strategies for individuals from diverse backgrounds.[59] As will become evident when we discuss the topic further later on in this book, for the behavioral and psychiatric outcomes we study, there is nothing deterministic about genes. Most human traits and diseases are due to a combination of genetic and environmental factors, and understanding how these factors interact will allow us to develop targeted interventions to optimize outcomes. More on this later, we now return to the family's saga.

6

Living with the Olsens

(59 DAYS IN OUT-OF-HOME CARE)

It is an unseasonably cool day, more spring-like than summer. Discharge from the Safe Home is scheduled for two o'clock. Danielle's associate Shannon, a social worker case aide with shoulder-length wispy blonde hair rings the bell to the Safe Home and tells the staff member who lets her in that she is there to pick up Sylar and Samya. The bright sunlight makes it hard initially for Shannon to see the face of the woman who answers the door.

"The children need to be checked by the nurse before they are released. I was just going to look for the nurse. Come on in."

As Shannon walks in she sees two children sitting at the table in the kitchen with large black plastic garbage bags by their chairs. She introduces herself to Sylar and Samya with a handshake and a warm smile. The house is quiet because the other children at the Safe Home are on an outing.

"Are you excited about going to live with the Olsens?"

Sylar gives a monosyllabic affirmative response. Samya does not speak; both children look up at Shannon briefly then avert their gaze down toward the floor.

Shannon sits down at the table kitty-corner to Samya. "I hear nice things about the Olsens. You went for a visit last weekend, didn't you?"

"Yep." As she replies, Samya thinks about the Olsen's home. It was a whole house, not just an apartment. When she first saw the zebra skin rug in the living room it freaked her out, but by the end of the weekend the rug and all the little African statues began to grow on her.

"There aren't any other children in the home, are there?"

"None that live there, but they have a fourteen-year-old grandson Tyrell who visits a lot."

Sylar then chimes in with a broad smile; "She beat his butt in basketball."

"Do they have a basketball hoop at their house?"

"Yeah—and a Nintendo PlayStation 2."

Samya then adds that they will each have their own bedrooms at the Olsen home, and the two of them will have their own bathroom to share.

Shannon replies, "That's going to be a nice change after living here with about a dozen kids and having to share just a few bathrooms." She then asks, "Did you do anything special when you visited last weekend?"

"We went to church and out to lunch. Sylar ate like a pig." Samya exchanges a teasing glance, and the two speak about all the food on the Chinese buffet where they went out to eat. They then move on to discussing an assortment of random topics to help pass the time.

It takes an hour for the staff to find the nurse, but at last the children are cleared and ready to go. They carry their bags out to the blue State car. The staff member from the Safe Home drives a different car and leads the way to the Olsen house, a 10-minute ride from the Safe Home. As they drive off, Samya looks out the rear window of the car, eyeing the white cottage as they drive away, and watching it grow smaller in the distance.

When they pull into the driveway, the children notice Mrs. Olsen standing on the stoop by the front door. She smiles as the children walk out of the car. A tall dark teenage boy comes out of the house behind her; Shannon assumes it is her grandson Tyrell. Warm, but cautious greetings are exchanged, and the children bound up the stairs behind Tyrell to their second-floor bedrooms. Shannon shares information with Mrs. Olsen about upcoming doctor appointments, and before she leaves she tells the children to behave.

Three weeks pass and the family's case is transferred to Carly (DCF-W6; Scott, DCF-W5, only worked with the family briefly while investigating the educational neglect allegations). As Carly drives up to the Olsen home for a visit, she sees who she guesses to be Sylar and Samya on the sidewalk holding the arms of Mrs. Olsen, who is gliding awkwardly on a pair of roller skates. She smiles; their laughter is contagious and the scene is really quite comical. Carly gets out of her car and introduces herself to Mrs. Olsen and the children. Mrs. Olsen explains that the children were teaching her to skate. Mrs. Olsen remarks, "One is never too old to learn new things."

Mrs. Olsen takes off the skates and she and Carly go into the house to talk. The children go out back. When Carly sits down in the kitchen she notices some photographs lying on the table. "Can I take a look?"

"Sure. Those are from our family reunion in New Jersey two weekends ago."

"You have a big family. It looks like there was a lot of food. Are people line-dancing in this shot?"

"Yes; and Samya can really dance. My family enjoyed meeting the children."

"Where are these pictures from?"

"We have a timeshare down in Virginia Beach. We took Sylar, Samya, and our grandson down for a vacation last week. You can see all three children in this picture riding in the bumper cars."

"It looks like they had a blast."

"They did, except neither Sylar nor Samya had any interest in swimming in the ocean."

After catching up on how things are going, and discussing upcoming plans for a court-ordered interactional assessment with the children and their mother, Carly goes out back to meet with the children.

The children sit at the picnic table on the back porch and talk about their trips and how things are going at the foster home. Sylar does most of the talking; Samya is quiet, mulling over her conversation with their mom during the last family visit. Shannon had driven them to the local McDonald's, where they met with their mom and Joseph. The image of her mom crying while waving goodbye as they drove away flashes through her mind.

Oblivious and indifferent to what Sylar and Carly are talking about, Samya blurts out, "My mom said we're going home after the next court hearing at the end of the month."

Carly responds, "Nothing is decided for sure. The Court decides if and when you go home."

"My mom said if we pass the test, we'll be going home."

"It's not a test that is coming up. It's called an interactional assessment. You, Sylar, and your mom will meet together with a psychologist to evaluate how you all get along. The court requested the evaluation to help them decide if your mom is ready for you to go home. The evaluation is scheduled for Monday, and I'll pick you up and take you there."

Carly does not tell the children that the Department is going to recommend to the court that the children stay in placement, but there is something about Carly's tone that crushes Samya's hopes of going home. Samya begins to cry, gets up, and leaves the table abruptly without saying a word. The back door flies wide open as she rushes into the house.

Mrs. Olsen tries to approach Samya, but Samya says she just wants to be alone. Samya sprints up the stairs to her bedroom. Carly leaves shortly thereafter, confirming an 11:30 pick up time for the interactional assessment on the following Monday.

Although the psychologist writes up a positive evaluation, the Court commits the children to the custody of the Department of Children and Families, making them wards of the state. There remains a carrot of hope that they might go home, however; the Court mandates an interactional assessment with Joseph to further evaluate the appropriateness of the children returning to their mother's care.

Carly picks the children up for this second interactional assessment, too. It takes place three weeks after the interactional assessment with Maria. Carly transports them first to the DCF office, where they stop to pick up Maria and Joseph on their way to the psychologist's office. When they get to the DCF office, the children get out of the van to greet their mother and Joseph. Samya gives her mother a necklace and rectangular cloth box; Sylar gives Joseph a silver chain with a medal and purple tassel. He also gives his mother five dollars. When Carly asks the children where they got these things, they say their foster mother gave it to them. She is concerned the things are stolen and plans to confirm the children's explanation with Mrs. Olsen.

Joseph goes to the men's room when they first arrive at the psychologist's office. While he is gone Maria pulls the children aside and quietly tells them that Joseph is abusing her again. The lighthearted expressions that characterized the start of the day fade. Before much more can be said, Joseph and the psychologist come to the waiting room. It is time for the evaluation; the children follow solemnly behind Joseph as they walk into the office.

While they are in the assessment, Maria elaborates on the situation. "It's getting dangerous. Joseph got arrested last week for beating me up and getting in a fight with a guy when he was out at a bar. He threatened to kill me."

Carly offers to find a shelter for Maria. She says Maria does not have to go back home with Joseph. She suggests that Maria come with her to the DCF office so they can find a place for her to go without Joseph knowing. Maria does not take her up on the offer. The atmosphere is tense and uncomfortable during and after the interactional assessment. Joseph feels the chill and at times stares down Maria and Sylar.

After dropping off Maria and Joseph at the DCF office, Carly takes Sylar and Samya back to their respective schools. They stop for lunch along the way, but both children barely touch their meals. No one speaks about what transpired.

Over the next few days, school and the Olsens keep the children busy and distracted from worries about their mother's safety. They each just started meeting with a tutor two days a week, both are signed up for basketball through the parks and recreation program, Sylar has flag football one afternoon a week, and Samya just started to sing with the church choir.

The weekend after the interactional assessment with Joseph, the Olsens' grandson Tyrell also comes to stay. His parents are out of town so he is with the Olsens from Friday night through Monday morning. It is a busy weekend.

Sunday night, Samya awakens to the feel of her brother's hand on the small of her back. The pressure of his hand brings her out of a deep sleep. Samya slowly lifts her head, squints her eyes, and takes in the blackness outside the window across from her bed. She is not sure what time it is, but she guesses it is many hours until dawn.

Sylar is talking to her as she first gets up, but she has no idea what he is saying. She rolls over and sits up, pulling her knees to her chest. It is then that she notices Tyrell standing behind her brother alternating between looking down at her and down at the ground.

Sylar continues to talk and she begins to register what is going on. Slowly his words come into focus. "Do you want to have sex with Tyrell?"

Samya replays her interactions with Tyrell from the day before. She and Tyrell sat next to each other when they went out for lunch after church. He was kinda flirting with her, and later in the day when they played basketball, she got a positive vibe from him.

She looks up at Tyrell and notices he is now looking down at the ground while Sylar outlines the plans. Sylar says he will stand guard by the door and exits the room, leaving the two of them alone. When Sylar closes the door, it is pitch black in her bedroom.

Tyrell then sits on the edge of her bed. Tyrell says something to her, but the lightheartedness that characterized their interactions earlier in the day is gone. Samya tries to look at Tyrell's face to see his expression, but it is too dark.

Samya feels him begin to grope her breasts. His hand is cold. She lays back. His dick is sticking outside his boxers, and she feels it brush against her leg as he stretches out on her bed. He pulls off her panties and fumbles about for a bit before he pushes inside her.

Samya listens to Tyrell groan, and she wraps her arms tight around him. His body is warm now, and it feels good to have him rocking on top of her. It isn't long until he collapses and rolls over. She wonders, *Am I his girlfriend now?*

Tyrell lies on his back by her side long enough to catch his breath, and then he turns to her and says, "I'll see you tomorrow." He then gets up and goes across the hall into Sylar's room.

After Tyrell leaves, Samya is surprised to find she is thinking about her mother, and how much she misses her. She begins to cry, and cries herself to sleep fighting away doubts about what just happened.

The next day at school Samya goes to the nurse's office and tells the nurse about Tyrell. She and Tyrell did not use protection, and she is worried about getting pregnant. The nurse calls Carly, who takes Samya to the pediatric sexual abuse clinic, where she is prescribed the morning after pill to prevent pregnancy and an antibiotic to prevent any sexually transmitted diseases.

Samya dreads what is next—going home to talk with Mrs. Olsen. She is sitting near Carly when she calls Mrs. Olsen to tell her what happened, but she cannot hear what Mrs. Olsen says.

When she gets back to the house, she is glad Carly is with her, and that Mr. Olsen is still at work. To Samya's surprise, Mrs. Olsen is not mad at her.

"I don't blame you. I blame myself. I feel like I let you kids down."

Carly suggests that Tyrell not visit for a while. "No worries," Mrs. Olsen assures her. She then explains that her daughter-in-law is livid and said it will be a good long time before she allows him back at the house.

Carly asks Mrs. Olsen if she wants the children removed because of this incident. Samya holds her breath and looks down toward the ground while she waits for Mrs. Olsen to reply.

"I don't think so. We've come to really love the kids. We'll have to see how things play out with the family, but I don't think so."

Samya looks up at Mrs. Olsen with an expression somewhere between relief and disbelief.

Carly then makes plans to come back the next day to talk with Sylar and Samya again and see how things are going. Before leaving, she asks Mrs. Olsen about the gifts the children had given to their mother and Joseph when they saw them at the interactional assessment.

Mrs. Olsen knows exactly the items the worker is describing, and she is surprised the children found them. They were stored away in a box in the back of the hallway closet.

"That medal belonged to my son who died in the war." Mrs. Olsen's voice cracks as she says this, and she has to work to keep her composure.

When Carly comes to the house the next day, they meet in the living room. Sylar and Samya sit close to one another on the couch; Mrs. Olsen and Carly sit on the two stuffed chairs facing them. Sylar and Samya frequently look at one another throughout the meeting. With their glances, they seal a pack of silence about the past. Both children are relieved to hear Mrs. Olsen say that she and Mr. Olsen want to move on and put this incident behind them.

Just when Sylar and Samya think they have made it through the worst of the morning, Carly reaches in her bag and pulls out the Medal of Honor and other things she had gotten back from Maria and Joseph. Mrs. Olsen's eyes water as she takes the things from Carly. There is a long and tense moment of silence. Sylar and Samya look briefly at one another, then down at the zebra-skin rug.

Mrs. Olsen addresses them both. In a slightly stern voice she says, "I want you two to look at me."

They both look up. The feeling of relief from just moments earlier is gone.

She goes on to say, "I understand stealing can be a way of survival, but you have to understand, it is wrong. You hurt other people when you steal, and you hurt yourself."

Sylar apologizes then surprises himself with what he says next. He talks briefly about a few of the many times he and Samya were asked by their mother to steal things. He can tell by the look in Samya's eyes that she is not mad at him for divulging this piece of their past.

Mrs. Olsen's voice softens. "When you make mistakes, you must learn from them, and then move on." Both children get up from the couch and give Mrs. Olsen a hug. Carly then leaves.

Shortly after this meeting, Sylar and Samya begin to call Mrs. and Mr. Olsen "Ma" and "Dad." For a few weeks it is back to business as usual. Their routine is predictable—school, chores, homework, extra curricular activities, tutoring twice a week, church, and Sunday lunch at the local Chinese buffet. They have basketball games almost every week, and the Olsens never miss a game. Much of their time is structured, but they still have free time; they are allowed to use the PlayStation 2 from five to six o'clock each night, or go out back and play basketball any time they want, if all their homework and chores are done.

The calm comes to an abrupt halt during one supervised phone call with their mother. Maria is on the phone in the DCF office. The children are speaking to her via speakerphone in the kitchen with Mrs. Olsen sitting beside them.

"Last night Joseph hit me in the face with a belt and ... "

Carly quickly interrupts Maria and redirects the dialogue, "That's not an appropriate topic of conversation. Why don't you ask the kids about school?"

After the phone call Maria told Carly that Joseph almost killed her the night before. He hit her in the head with his belt, and then wrapped it around her neck until she passed out. He kept her locked in the bedroom, watching her the whole time, even when she went to the bathroom.

Carly arranges to take Maria to a shelter that night, but she is back with Joseph less than a week later. It takes another incident in which he nearly kills her, and for which he is incarcerated, for Maria to completely end that relationship. In the weeks that follow, at the end of each supervised telephone call, Sylar asks to speak to Carly. He then inquires, "Is my mom *really* OK? Is Joseph still locked up?"

Around the same time the violence gets out of control between Maria and Joseph, the police arrest Sylar and Tyrell on charges of risk of injury to a minor because of the sexual encounter with Samya that occurred the month prior. Tyrell attends juvenile court with his mother; Carly accompanies Sylar. Both boys are terrified, but reassured to learn that the charges will be dropped if they complete counseling. Tyrell begins counseling immediately. Because DCF is Sylar's legal guardian, he needs DCF to get him into treatment. Mr. and Mrs. Olsen have no authority to do this. There is a therapist who works with the family from the foster care agency, but she is not a specialist in this area.

A month later, Sylar is still not in counseling, and the idea of referring the children for treatment comes to the forefront again after Samya gets in trouble for giving a sexually provocative note to a 10-year-old boy at her school. There is more talk by Carly and her supervisor about referring the children for specialized counseling, but again the referral is still not initiated.

Other than the one incident when Samya wrote the inappropriate note to the boy at school, things at school are going well for the children. When their fall report cards arrive in the mail, Mrs. Olsen calls them into the kitchen and hands them each the envelope containing their grades. After ripping the envelope open and quietly staring at the page, a smile erupts across Sylar's face. He cannot remember another time he felt so proud. He has all A's and B's. Samya is close behind with only one C on her report card. The behavior comments are good, too. Both children are described as respectful and helpful in the classroom. After reading the report cards with Sylar and Samya watching anxiously, Mrs. Olsen gives both children a hug and says, "These are great! We'll have to show them to Mr. Olsen when he gets home. I think a trip to Friendly's is in order after dinner to celebrate!"

Samya's one C was in history. In that class, she has an oral report coming up the following week on Aphrodite. She asks Mrs. Olsen if Mrs. Olsen can help her make a costume for her presentation, because some of the other kids wore costumes when they gave their presentations. Over the next week the two work together on the costume, first going together to the fabric store to get material, then drafting the design and pattern together. Mrs. Olsen does the machine sewing; Samya helps with the handwork. The night before her presentation, Samya gets into full costume and practices giving her report in front of Sylar and Mr. and Mrs. Olsen. By the second run through she is fluid, and she evidently does a great job in front of her class, because she earns a solid A on the project.

Things continue along smoothly at the foster home, but December is a busy month. It starts with a big event at a church in town where Mrs. Olsen's cousin is pastor. A choir from a church in North Carolina is coming up for a gospel weekend. There will be a big performance at the church with a special reception to follow. Regular Sunday clothes are not good enough for this event so both children go shopping for new things to wear. To find the perfect out-fit, Samya and Mrs. Olsen go to three different stores. After getting her hair straightened and getting ready in her new dress and patent leather pumps with one-inch heals, Samya looks at herself in the mirror beaming ear to ear. She then flits downstairs and finds Mr. Olsen in the living room, and shows off her new outfit with a spin. Remembering her conversation with him from when they first met at the Safe Home, she says, "Now I really do feel like a Princess!"

The euphoria from the gospel performance weekend is short-lived. Soon after, Sylar and Samya learn from Carly that their mother is in a new relation-ship. Both are worried. They are not told that she is treated at the ER after an incident of domestic violence, or that she tests positive for cocaine while she is there, but they have a growing feeling that their return home is not com-ing any time soon. They also are feeling more and more comfortable with the Olsens, and do not mind staying where they are while their mother continues to flounder.

The Olsens feel the children growing closer to them, but they also appreci-ate the strength of their bond with their mother. As Christmas time nears, they give both children $20 to buy some special gifts for their mother. The week before Christmas, DCF schedules a special two-hour holiday visit for the chil-dren with their mother. The children have the day off from school, so they are supposed to get picked up at noon to be brought to the DCF office where the visit is scheduled to take place. Both Sylar and Samya put on the outfits they wore to the gospel festival. At a few minutes past noon, Sylar starts waiting outside, gifts in hand. It is raining, but he wants to be ready the moment the case aide arrives to transport them to the visit. By 12:30 Mrs. Olsen starts call-ing the DCF office to find out why no one has arrived, and she calls regularly for the next several hours. No one picks up the telephone and no one returns her call, and Mrs. Olsen cannot get Sylar in from the rain. He is soaked and crying, but determined to be ready when the aide arrives. Finally Mrs. Olsen calls Mr. Olsen and asks him to come home early from work. It is almost five o'clock by the time he gets to the house and is at last able to persuade Sylar to come inside.

Sylar spends most of that night sobbing in his room. He cries for all the times his mother disappointed him and for his lost belief that things can change. Samya keeps to herself, listening to music through headphones in her room. She does not want to allow herself to experience the reality that is crashing down on Sylar.

The next family visit at McDonalds, Sylar does not hide his anger. When his mother tries to blame DCF for messing up the times of the visit, he confronts her.

"The last time we were together we talked about the upcoming Christmas visit. Face it, you messed up, you forgot."

Sylar walks away from the table before his mother has a chance to respond. Samya tries to compensate and is extra cheery with her mother. Sylar eventually sits back down at their table, but maintains an icy glare, refusing to engage in conversation. When Shannon announces that the visit is over, Sylar is up out of his chair and to the door in seconds. He does not look back, he does not say goodbye.

The children's next visit with their mother is canceled. They are not told why over the phone, but Carly says she will be by the next day to see them. Samya is worried; Sylar is still pissed.

When Carly arrives, they can tell something is wrong. She asks Mrs. Olsen to join them when they meet. They all sit at the kitchen table. Carly lets them know their mother is in the hospital. When she first says this Sylar and Samya imagine that their mom's new boyfriend beat her up. Their imaginations are wrong. Maria tried to kill herself. She is in a psychiatric hospital. Carly has not seen her yet, but says she will update the children when she does. There is more talk, but at this point, Sylar and Samya are lost in their own thoughts. Sylar feels guilty and thinks maybe he had been too hard on his mother. Samya is thinking that they have to get home. She thinks that their mother cannot make it on her own.

Visits are suspended after Maria is hospitalized. The children begin to open up and tell Mrs. and Mr. Olsen more about their past, but not everything. They talk about the many times they saw their mother beaten, and they let them know about the times they saw their mother sell sex for drugs. They talk about how they hate that their mother is an addict, and how they do not understand why their mother does drugs. They also openly start to question whether they want to go home. Their mother is discharged from the hospital after about a week. The children do not know she makes a second suicide attempt a week later and is readmitted to the hospital.

Between Maria's first and second suicide attempts, the children finally have an intake for counseling. It has been almost four months since the incident with Tyrell and Samya, and six months since the incident with Sabina and Sylar at the Safe Home. Tyrell's mother no longer lets him sleep over, but after he finished counseling she allowed Tyrell to come to the house for a few hours or to join them for lunch after church. Tyrell blames Samya for getting him in trouble and their friendship is never the same.

Mrs. Olsen goes to a few counseling sessions with Sylar and Samya. She likes Samya's therapist well enough at first, but things sour between them. Mrs. Olsen is not sure whether it is related, but she thinks things changed when the two women realized they came from the same small town back in North Carolina. Both their families had been farmers, and both had lost their farms, but many whites from the area blamed the black sharecroppers and their migration north for their family's misfortune. Mrs. Olsen supports the children's involvement in treatment, despite the antagonistic relationship between her and Samya's therapist.

After a month of no visits, Mr. Olsen calls Carly and says he does not think the visits should be restarted. The children are opening up and talking more and more about their experiences before coming into care. He is afraid if the visits are restarted, the children will shut down.

The day after this conversation with Mr. Olsen, as if it never happened, Carly calls to schedule a supervised telephone call with Maria. Visits are then restarted the following week. On the way to the first visit the children ask Shannon, who is driving them, to stop at a store. They each buy snacks, and Sylar buys a red rose for his mother. Once at the DCF office, both children greet their mother warmly. Sylar hands her the rose. As they move into the visitation room the flow of conversation comes easily, but after a period of time, Sylar moves to the corner of the room and sits with his legs up and his head on his knees. Maria asks him multiple times if he is OK, and each time he replies with one word, "Yes." Samya and her mother chat about school, music, and all sorts of different things, ignoring Sylar. When the hour is up, Samya hugs her mother long and tight and tells her that she loves her. Sylar quickly embraces his mother, but does not look at her face as he says goodbye.

The next several times they see their mother, Sylar and Samya take turns being sullen during the visits. It is not intentional; it is just happens. Samya also gets in a fight with the Olsens. She wants to go to a party at her friend's house, but the Olsens forbid her to go. They never explain why, but they did not want her to go to the party because they know the girl's parents use and sell drugs. They know it is the type of home where anything can happen. The week after she misses the party Samya goes into therapy and complains to her counselor about being restricted due to the incident that occurred with Tyrell. She also says it is uncomfortable when Tyrell is at the house because he blames her for his getting in trouble, and she asserts that the Olsens hold her responsible for that incident.

After listening to Samya's complaints, the therapist calls Carly and recommends that the children be removed from the foster parents' home. No one ever speaks to the Olsens to express their concerns. Ten years after the children's removal, I asked Mrs. Olsen if she thought Samya was to blame for the encounter with her grandson. It took her less than a nanosecond to say she held herself and her grandson responsible. She felt guilty that it happened under her roof, and she went on to say that she had repeatedly spoken to her grandson about the negatives of unprotected sex and sex before the appropriate age. She did not falter in her conviction.

Two days after the telephone call from Samya's therapist, there is a meeting between Carly and staff from the private foster care agency to discuss the therapist's recommendation. The Olsens are not included in the meeting. Carly, based on the therapists' recommendation and her concerns that Tyrell is visiting in the home, questions the safety of having the children remain with the Olsens. The director and the foster care agency representative who has been working with the Olsens support the children's ongoing placement with the Olsens.

"The children are thriving. Sylar is participating in basketball and flag football, and Samya is participating in basketball, choir, and dance."

The director of the private foster care agency thinks the issues can be worked out and comments that the Olsens are dedicated and loving foster parents. She is supposed to set up a meeting with the Olsens, but that meeting never occurs. Had the Olsens been at the table they would likely have said that they thought it was OK for their grandson to start visiting in the home again after he completed treatment and all the charges were dropped. They would have let them know that Tyrell's mother no longer lets him sleep over, and they would have likely reminded Carly that they were Tyrell's grand mommy and grand pap. They also might have shared their concerns about Samya's friend's family and explained why they restricted her activities in that instance—not overall. They also would have talked about how much they have come to love the children, and how the children had begun to really open up to them. This conversation, however, never takes place.

Ten days after the meeting between Carly and the foster care agency executive director, Carly goes to visit Samya at her school and asks her whether she feels she is restricted unfairly, blamed for the incident that occurred in the fall, and unsafe because Tyrell is back in the home. Samya is still mad about not getting to go to her friend's party, so she answers, "Yes," to all of the above. Carly then asks her if she wants to leave the foster home. She says she does—and a part of her does want to leave. And not just because she is mad about not getting to go to the party. She feels guilty about growing close to the Olsens, worried about her mom, and is afraid if she stays there even longer, she will never get home. These are thoughts and fears, however, which never get discussed.

After meeting with Samya, Carly goes to Sylar's school to talk with him. He says he will do whatever Samya wants. He wants to be with his sister.

At 3:15 in the afternoon, Mrs. Olsen glances at the clock anticipating the children's arrival from school. By 3:20 she thinks it curious that the children are not yet home. That sense of wonder turns to worry. At four o'clock she calls the school. No one knows anything. At 4:15 Mrs. Olsen starts to call the police, but decides to call the local DCF child welfare office. At last, she gets some information. Sylar and Samya were picked up from school and brought to the Meriden DCF office—but why? No further information is provided. Mrs. Olsen calls the Meriden DCF office. No one answers the telephone. She leaves several messages. Not until nine o'clock that night does a case supervisor call Mrs. Olsen to say DCF is taking the children out of her home "for a while." The supervisor says DCF thinks it "best at this time." No further information is provided. Mr. and Mrs. Olsen are both sad and confused, but want what is "best" for the children. No one follows up to discuss things with the Olsens.

It is noted in the DCF record that the placement "fell through partly due to poor scheduling of a much needed meeting and lack of communication."

Placement Disruption

Placement changes or disruptions, unfortunately, are a frequent and accepted practice in child welfare. The federal government standard definition of *adequate placement stability* is "limiting the number of placement settings for a child to no more than two for a single foster care episode."[60]

The greatest majority of placement changes are due to administrative reasons; children like Sylar and Samya being moved from a short-term shelter to a foster home, children being moved from a foster placement to a relative's home, or moves so siblings can be together.[61] The longer children are in foster care, however, the greater the likelihood of placement changes. Nationally, the federal standard of two or fewer placements is met for approximately 85% of the children in care less than a year, approximately 64% of the children in care 12–24 months, and only 35% of the children in care longer than two years.[60] One large-scale study of foster care alumni reported that approximately one-third of the youth experienced eight or more placements.[62]

The second most common reason for placement changes is children's behavior problems; it is estimated that approximately 20% of placements disrupt due to children's problematic behavior.[63] In recognition of this, a number of effective interventions have been developed to address children's behavior problems at time of placement.[64] (See Reference 64 for the website to download an article that reviews the most effective programs.)

Behavior problems, however, are not only a cause of placement disruption, but a consequence of placement disruption.[65] Although children entering care with more problems are more likely to disrupt from placement, children without significant difficulties at placement who are moved around develop problems. This unfortunately will be vividly illustrated in the coming chapter.

Nevertheless, Sylar and Samya's placement did not fail due to their behavior problems. Mr. and Mrs. Olsen were quite accepting of the children's misbehaviors; they did not reject them after they were caught stealing priceless things that belonged to their deceased son, or when their behaviors caused strife with the extended family. They were loving and intrinsically skilled in providing structure and helping to bring out the best in the children.

What other factors predict placement disruption? Characteristics of the surrogate parents, such as having fostered more children, and having a lower level of commitment to the children in the home also predict placement disruption.[66] In addition, placements with a greater number of children in the home, especially when the children are unrelated, tend to be less stable.[67] These factors will be relevant later in our story, but they do not apply to circumstances at the Olsen's home.

Greater worker turnover, and weak foster parent–worker relationships are two other factors associated with increased risk for placement failure.[67] These factors likely contributed to this instance of placement disruption. As noted in the DCF case record, the placement "fell through partly due to poor scheduling of a much needed meeting and lack of communication."

Over the past decade and a half a number of child welfare mediation programs have been developed around the country.[68] Mediators specially trained in child welfare issues are engaged to facilitate constructive communication and devise creative solutions among conflicting parties involved in child protective services cases. It is not the whole case that is referred for mediation, just a specific issue (e.g., services, relationship issues, visitation, or conditional surrender of rights). Most child welfare mediation programs focus on conflicts between birth parents and the State. More recently, specialized programs have been developed to mediate complaints concerning the rights of foster parents and concerns about the action, inaction, or decisions of the child-placing agency.[68] Although formal mediation might not have been necessary in the case with the Olsens, it is a travesty that there was never any direct communication with the Olsens before the children were removed from their home. In a snapshot view of a case, the long-term ramifications of a given decision are not always evident. The consequences of this placement failure were far reaching, but I am getting ahead of myself. Let's return to the story and you will see for yourself how things unfold.

7

Five Placements in Five Weeks

(291 DAYS IN OUT-OF-HOME CARE)

The late afternoon sunlight streams in through the window in the room at the Meriden DCF office with the couches with the wooden armrests, the TV, and the VCR—the room where Sylar and Samya had waited two times before to learn where they would be going next. They are watching an afternoon sitcom and sitting side by side in silence. Both are lost in their own thoughts. Sylar has an ache in the pit of his stomach. Samya hopes she has done the right thing.

Carly is across the hall in her cubicle talking on the telephone with the director of the Safe Home at the treatment center where the children were placed before they went to live with the Olsens.

"We do have two beds available, but I'm not sure we can have Sylar back given what happened the last time he was here."

"What happened the last time he was there?"

"One night he crawled in the bed of a female client. He had his pajamas on when she screamed and he was caught. There was only that one instance, but we kept a close eye on him after that. I'd feel more comfortable readmitting him if I could have some assurances from someone who's been working with him clinically."

"Let me see if I can get his therapist on the phone. I'll call you back."

Carly is able to get Dr. Worth, Sylar's new therapist, on the telephone. He also had not known about the incident that occurred at the Safe Home. He says he has only met with Sylar a few times and does not feel he can give a definitive recommendation, especially with this new information about the incident that occurred at the Safe Home. After discussing the options, he says, "It might be best to err on the side of caution and place Sylar in a home with only males and with no children younger than twelve. That will reduce the risk of anything happening."

Carly calls the director of the Safe Home back and arranges for Samya's placement—only Samya. She says she will arrange transportation for her, and Samya will likely be arriving at the Safe Home within the next hour. She lets the director know that Samya is still enrolled in the same school she started when she was at the Safe Home last spring, and that she will need some things, as she has no clothes or toiletries with her.

Carly then goes to talk with the children. She is vague. She says there is only one spot available at the Safe Home where they were last, and that Samya will be going there. A case aide will drive her. The din of the TV in the background dulls their senses. *Did she just say we are going to be separated?* Sylar's heart is pounding and his ears are ringing. Before there can be any further discussion, the case aide comes in the room, ready to drive Samya to the Safe Home. Sylar watches as Samya walks out the door and down the long corridor; Samya turns and looks back at Sylar multiple times as she ambles hesitantly toward the exit.

Carly explains what will happen next, but Sylar cannot comprehend a word of the conversation. Carly then goes back across the hallway to make phone calls from her cubby, and Sylar is alone in the room with the couches with the wooden armrests. He sits staring at the TV with his knees curled into his chest.

After about half an hour, Carly brings some snacks in for Sylar. She says, "I think I found you a home for tonight. I just need to talk with my supervisor. I'll be back in a bit."

There is a 12-year old girl in the home, but Carly's supervisor approves the placement on a temporary basis because all efforts to find a home with no females and no children under 12 failed. A television show later she is back and they are ready to go.

The home Carly found for Sylar is not far from the DCF office. Sylar sits in the backseat of the blue State car and stares out the window as they drive there, too tired to make any conversation. They drive past the McDonald's where Sylar's mom probably got the food she brought to the visits at the Safe Home, past a small lake, and then they make a left turn onto a side road. They stop at the first house on the right. It is a modest two-story tan cottage-style home with brown shutters and a porch by the front door that wraps around the side of the house facing the lake. There is no one on the porch to welcome him like when he moved to the Olsen's home.

Sylar follows behind Carly as she climbs up the wooden steps to the front door. He has his backpack slung over his shoulder. He stops and looks across the roadway to the lake. There is a lake by the Safe Home. He wishes he were there with Samya.

Carly introduces Sylar to Mrs. C. She lets Mrs. C. know that a case aide will be by in the morning to pick Sylar up to take him to school. It will be almost an hour ride, so the aide will be by early. Sylar is introduced to Mrs. C's daughter and another foster boy about his age who also lives in the home. He does not remember either of their names.

The night passes slowly. Sylar is not sure whether he ever falls asleep. The next day he sees his sister at the child guidance center during their therapy sessions. Whenever they were at the clinic before, they left together. Now two separate case aides are waiting for them to drive them to their respective placements. When Samya gets back to the Safe Home she asks the director to call Carly and arrange for telephone contact with Sylar. She is not happy to be separated from him. Neither is happy with the current arrangements.

Two days later the children have a supervised visit with their mother at the Meriden DCF office. Midway through the visit Carly enters the room.

"Sylar, you have an interview for a new foster home after the visit tonight."

Sylar gets a surprised look on his face; he is not sure why he might be moving. Before he can ask any questions, Maria barks, "Why is he being interviewed for another foster home? And how come my kids aren't together?" Carly explains the first home was only temporary. Sylar and Samya both chime in with complaints, but Carly cuts off the discussion and tries to calm the mood.

"You have to be patient with the process and trust things will all work out. Don't waste the rest of the time you have together arguing about this. There is another visit scheduled in just a few days; we can discuss updates then. I know this is hard on everyone."

With those remarks, Carly leaves the room. Maria and the children then pass the last half-hour of the visit playing Pictionary.

The first new placement Carly found for Sylar fell through. She identifies another home, but there are five girls in the home; two 9-year-olds, two 11-year-olds, and one 16-year-old. The foster mother says she can keep Sylar over the weekend, but not any longer because she does not accept children who require high structure. There are no other options. It will have to do for a few days.

Sylar's second temporary foster home is also in Meriden, just a bit farther out of town than the last home. Sylar sits in the back seat of the car as Carly drives him to this placement. They turn off the main thoroughfare of town, down a winding road, and past a farm with two horses grazing in the field. They then turn into a development that was likely built in the 1960s. The street is lined with cedar-sided split-level raised ranches. It is the type of development that if you turn yourself around, you can easily get lost. Except for variation in color, all the homes are identical. Midway up the block Carly turns into a driveway of a white split-level ranch with black shutters. Sylar notices a portable basketball hoop set up in the front of the yard by the street. An image of the basketball hoop in the Olsen's backyard flashes through Sylar's mind.

When they get out of the car, Sylar again follows Carly up the steps to the front door with his school backpack slung over his shoulder. He is greeted by Mrs. H. His head is spinning while she reviews the house rules: no swearing, no stealing, no going into the girls' rooms, and no walking around the home in pajamas. Sylar nods agreeably and tries to smile and maintain eye contact with Mrs. H. He fights the urge to go back to the car and curl up on the back seat. Carly lets Mrs. H. know that a case aide will be by to pick Sylar up for school early on Monday morning.

The weekend passes quickly. Mrs. H. is friends with Mrs. D. who lives down the street. Mrs. D. is also a foster mother. She has four boys living in her home. After church on Sunday the two families have lunch together. Sylar has a reasonable day on Sunday; lunch after church is a familiar routine.

Monday morning Carly gets a call from Sylar's therapist. He will not have his recommendations ready in time for the next court hearing. He also lets her know that Samya will be getting a new therapist because her therapist left the clinic. He then adds that he is not sure he is comfortable with Samya's old therapist's recommendations. He says he needs to review the case further.

Later in the day Carly gets a phone call from Sylar's school nurse. Sylar is sick. Shannon, who is scheduled to pick him up at the end of the day for his visit with his mom, comes to school early and picks him up a bit after one o'clock. Sylar curls up in the back seat of the car while they wait for Samya to get out of school.

"What hurts?"

"My head and my throat are killing me."

"We'll get something for you when we get to the DCF office."

On the car ride to the Meriden DCF office, the children bicker.

"If you had kept your mouth shut I would have a place to live now."

"I don't understand why you just can't be at the Safe Home with me."

"I messed up when I was there; they probably don't want me back."

After a moment of silence Samya asks Shannon, "Can you turn the music up?" She then asks for it to be turned even louder. The music fills the car and the children do not talk any more for the remainder of the ride.

Sylar spends much of the visit curled into a ball lying on the couch. Maria initially dotes over him then lets him lie undisturbed. Samya has some pictures with her that she shows her mother. When Maria asks if she can keep some of the photographs, Samya teases, "No, you'll just lose them."

When the visit is over, Sylar accompanies Samya on the ride back to the Safe Home. Sylar sleeps most of the way; Samya listens to music and sings with the radio. Shannon then brings Sylar back to the DCF office for another change in placement.

Carly drives Sylar to his new foster home; his third since leaving the Olsens one week ago. This is Mrs. D.'s home. Carly notes that Sylar appears a bit timid around the other males in the home. She exchanges information with Mrs. D. and lets Sylar know she will check in with him next week during his visit with his mother.

When Carly checks in with Sylar at the end of the family visit the following week Sylar says, "I'm not going back there tonight. I'll run away if you make me go."

Maria is upset that Sylar has been moving around so much, and the conversation escalates. Carly's supervisor comes to the family visit room to attempt to calm things down. After Maria and Samya leave, Carly talks one on one with Sylar to try to understand his complaints.

"Are there particular things you don't like at Mrs. D.'s home? Has anything happened?"

"It's too noisy in that house. I can't concentrate and do my homework, and one of the kids broke my Dragon Ball Z figure."

Sylar then discusses a litany of other complaints ranging from not being allowed to eat after school until dinnertime to complaining about having to go to church three times per week. Carly encourages him to try to salvage the placement, and she calls the family to discuss Sylar's concerns. Sylar agrees to give it another try, but the family changes their mind in the 20 minutes it takes Sylar and Carly to get to the house. The other kids in the house have a lot of questions, and Carly notes Sylar looks embarrassed as he packs up his things and prepares to leave.

On their way back to the office, Carly gets Sylar some dinner. While she tries to locate another temporary foster home, Sylar passes the time in the room with the TV, VCR, and couches with the wooden armrests.

At about nine o'clock, they pull into the pebbled driveway of temporary foster home number four. Sylar is not sure how far they have driven because he fell asleep in the car on the way to this new placement.

When Sylar gets into the car with the case aide the next morning to leave for school, it is not quite light out. He runs the events of the previous night through his head. He briefly remembers following Carly to the front door of the house and being introduced to a bunch of people, but he really cannot remember the faces of the people he met, or any of their names. He sleeps on the ride to school, and he feels a bit like an automaton as he goes about his day.

Carly calls Mrs. M. in the morning.

"It took Sylar a bit to settle in, but he is funny and rather charming."

Carly lets Mrs. M. know that this is just a temporary placement and she reviews the safety issues involved because there are two girls in the home. Mrs. M. lets her know that Sylar has his own room and that males and females are not allowed in one another's rooms. Neither are they allowed to watch television together without supervision. Mrs. M. says she has dealt with youth with similar issues before, and that Sylar can stay as long as is necessary—so long as no problems arise.

That day at three o'clock, the case aide picks up Sylar from school. They get in the blue State car, start driving immediately, and get off the highway at 4:20. Sylar has no idea where he is. He hopes the aide knows where they are going, because if she asks him to describe his new *home*, he cannot. Some of the homes they pass as they are driving along are huge, classic New England clapboard colonials. They pass some cows, a "horse crossing" sign, and a few farms. They also pass a Masonic temple; Mr. Olsen was a Freemason. Sylar's thoughts wander and he remembers the one time he went with Mr. Olsen to a meeting at the Masonic Temple. After a few minutes the case aide pulls into a gravel driveway with a green pickup truck parked in it. It is the most unkempt house on the street, a single-level ranch with a stone foundation and no paint on the siding.

The next day Sylar again leaves for school before the sun is up. Mrs. M. is not happy with the early start. When the DCF office opens several hours later, Mrs. M. calls Carly and says she is glad to keep Sylar as long as necessary, but this crack of dawn wake up schedule has to end. She wants him enrolled in the local school as soon as possible.

Before leaving the office that afternoon, Carly calls the foster home and asks to speak with Sylar. After inquiring about his day and how things are going at the new home she tells Sylar that he will be transferring to the local school the following day.

"But I just made the baseball team."

"You can try out for some teams at the new school. Your old school is just too far away."

"What about my girlfriend?"

"You'll make new friends."

The next morning, Carly comes to the house at about ten o'clock to enroll Sylar in the local school. As Sylar walks down the hallway of the local school with Carly, he feels people's eyes linger. At first he lowers his gaze, but then he looks back up. He is in a sea of white. The town Sylar lived in with the Olsens was 20% African American, and adjacent to a city that was almost 40% African American. This new town is less than 1% African American. Sylar is not sure he has the energy required to fit into a new school. As it turns out, this concern is irrelevant. Less than three weeks after he changes schools, a space opens up at a foster home in another part of the state. It can be a long-term placement, a home somewhat like a group home, designated for adolescent males with histories of sexual acting out behavior.

While Sylar is living with Mrs. M., he misses two visits with his mother and sister. Given the distance, it is too hard to coordinate the transportation. At the first visit Sylar misses, Samya is heard muttering under her breath, "Where the hell is my brother? This is bullshit." The second time she arrives at the DCF office for a visit with her mother and learns her brother is not coming, she begins to cry.

Two days before Sylar moves to the new long-term foster home, there is another court hearing regarding his risk of injury charges from the incident that occurred between Tyrell and Samya. Sylar has only seen Dr. Worth once since being removed from the Olsen's home so the evaluation is still not complete—nine months after the incident with Sabina, seven months since the incident with Samya, six months from the time the charges were filed, and four months after Tyrell completed treatment and had his charges dismissed.

The judge nulled the charges against Sylar on the terms that DCF complete the evaluation and follow through with whatever recommendations are made.

Sylar moves into his new long-term foster home on the day before his fourteenth birthday. It is his first birthday in care. He has no contact with any family members on his birthday, a pattern that repeats itself throughout his time in care. Carly takes him out to lunch at Friendly's before bringing him to his new placement, and takes him to Wal-Mart to pick out a present. He buys a new Dragon Ball Z toy.

During this period of transition and separation, both children think a lot about the Olsens. The Olsens also think regularly about the children, but if they could have glimpsed them in the two months that followed the children's removal from their home, they may not have recognized them.

By the time Sylar gets to his fifth and "permanent" foster placement, he has a short fuse. In one incident he is playing basketball with one of the boys at his new home when he loses it and starts choking the boy after the youth accidentally trips him. Sylar also develops problems with his hygiene. He is not bathing regularly.

Samya's fuse is also getting short. She is suspended twice from school. Once for storming out of the classroom and wandering around school grounds, and another time for cursing out a teacher. Around this same time, the school sends Carly a warning notice; Samya is at-risk of failing three of her courses—math, reading, and social studies.

The Safe Home staff also notice changes. One day Samya gets so upset about not having visits with her brother that she threatens to kill herself if she does not get to see him. Staff at the Safe Home also note that she is looking increasingly sad, so Samya is referred for an evaluation with the psychiatrist affiliated with the Safe Home. He diagnoses her with major depression and starts her on medication.

One afternoon during this particularly down period and after a month of not seeing Sylar, Samya walks in the school office expecting to see only Shannon there to drive her to the visit with her mother. She opens the door to the office absentmindedly, and seated next to Shannon she sees her *brother!* Samya drops her backpack by the door and runs to Sylar beaming. The two hug long and tight, then Sylar goes to the doorway and picks up Samya's back-pack. He carries it for her as they walk arm and arm to the car, talking face-to-face excitedly.

They sit together in the back of the car. Sylar tells Samya about his new foster home and his new school, and Samya tells Sylar about things at the Safe Home. The ride to Meriden passes quickly. When they walk in the DCF office, Maria squeals, "My babies are together!" The case aide then herds them into a visitation room. All are animated at the start of the visit, but as the hour advances, Sylar becomes somewhat withdrawn and sullen. This pattern repeats itself over the next two family visits. Sylar also starts to express overt anger toward his mother.

At one family visit he looks at his mother with disgust and asks, "When are you going to get a job and do what you got to do so we can come home?"

Maria looks hurt and replies, "Are you siding with DCF now?"

With an air of impatience Sylar says, "Just tell me. When are you going to do what you got to do so we can come home?"

Samya looks confused and asks Sylar, "Why are you so mad at Ma?"

"If you have to ask, you wouldn't understand."

Since being discharged from the hospital after her two suicide attempts, Maria did successfully complete a partial hospital treatment program. During the period of time when the kids were in transition, however, she was on a waiting list for a dual diagnosis outpatient program—a program that could address her mental health and addiction issues simultaneously. During this time frame, Carly notes in the record that Maria is not in treatment and she tested positive for using crack cocaine.

Given Maria's failure to make progress in completing the court required steps for reunification, and the impact of the brutal memories about domestic violence Samya starts to discuss in counseling, Samya's new therapist recommends visits between the children and their mother be suspended. Carly comes to the clinic to tell the children about the suspension of visits during one of their sessions. Sylar is silent as she speaks; Samya cries quietly without protesting.

In the interim, Carly finds a new foster home for Samya, but Samya is not yet up to visiting and meeting this new foster family. Carly gets permission for Samya to stay at the Safe Home until the end of the school year.

The children's first visits with one another without their mother are awkward. Shannon drives them and supervises the visits, and the children complain she never leaves them alone. Their first visit takes place at a Dunkin Donuts, the second visit is at the Safe Home, and from then on the visits are held at Sylar's foster home. Neither child is told that their mother is again admitted to the hospital for suicidality after visits are suspended.

When Samya first visits at Sylar's new foster home, it reminds her of the Safe Home. There is a white board on the kitchen wall that lists the chores of the eight boys in the home. There is also a rec room downstairs with an Xbox, a TV, and tons of board games. His foster mother, Marla, is not there in the afternoons; she works full-time. Her daughter is licensed as a day care provider and she and one other woman supervise the boys in the afternoon while Marla is at work. One of the two women frequently needs to drive one of the boys to a doctor or therapy appointment in the afternoons, and the other one stays at the house and watches the other boys. It is technically a foster home, but it feels more like a group home, with unrelated kids placed together and various staff on shift at different times.

The second time Samya comes for a visit at Sylar's foster home, it is the day before her thirteenth birthday—her second birthday in care. Shannon, who drove her, picked up some cupcakes to celebrate. Shannon keeps the cupcakes hidden in her car and lets Sylar know about them so he can come get them later and surprise Samya.

Sylar and Samya spend most of the visit in the backyard playing basketball. One of the boys from the house joins them for part of the time. Sylar talks about hoping to find a job for the summer; Samya talks about having spent the weekend at her new foster family's home. She says she likes them and she is looking forward to moving there next week. Sylar leaves for a few minutes and when he comes back he has a cupcake in his hand.

"Happy birthday to you. Happy birthday to you."

The other boy joins in and Samya blushes as they sing to her. The visit wraps up shortly after they finish their cupcakes. Sylar gives Samya a hug, wishes her a happy birthday again, and smiles warmly as she drives off down the winding road.

The day Samya moves to her "permanent" foster home, Dr. Worth submits his report to DCF. Sylar is not a sex offender; he is not a danger. Dr. Worth is planning on switching Sylar from group therapy to individual therapy to address his past history of sexual abuse. Sylar was severely abused, by multiple perpetrators, and exposed repeatedly to inappropriate sexual activity. Carly sits in her cubby reading the report. It started when he was five years old.

Problematic Sexualized Behavior in Children in the Child Welfare System

If this were a work of fiction and I decided to have the report from Dr. Worth arrive on the same day that Samya is placed in her new foster home and permanently separated from her brother, an editor might say it was too contrived, but as the expression goes, "the truth is stranger than fiction." After five moves and a two-and-a-half-month period of transition and uncertainty for both children, the verdict was in. Sylar was not a sexual offender. He had a history of horrendous sexual abuse, and when he first entered care, he had no idea what appropriate sexuality or interpersonal boundaries were.

Problematic sexualized behavior is common among children within the child welfare system, reported in approximately 11% of children in foster care, 17% of children in group care, and 30% of children in residential treatment settings.[69] In prior research studies, *problematic sexualized behavior* was defined as being above the clinical cut-off on a well-validated scale, the Child Sexual Behavior Inventory,[70] or the presence of one or more of the following intrusive behaviors: touches other child's sex parts, tries to have intercourse, puts mouth on sex parts, touches adult sex parts, touches animal sex parts, asks others to do sex acts, tries to look at people when they are nude or undressing, tries to undress other children, shows sex parts to children, or tries to undress adults against their will.[71]

Not surprisingly, among children in the child welfare system, problematic sexualized behavior is more common in children with histories of sexual abuse, and children like Sylar, who have had a host of other traumatic experiences.[71] Problematic sexualized behaviors also co-occur with other mental health problems, including PTSD, depression, and conduct disorder.[72] It is important to note, however, most sexually abused children do not offend against others.[73,74]

Although there is consensus that the true prevalence of child sexual abuse is unknown,[75] a synthesis of self-report studies suggest the best estimate is approximately 12% of adults were sexually abused by an adult as a child, with sexual abuse including everything from indecent touching of children on their private parts to penetrative sexual assaults.[72] When experiences of sexual assault and sexual abuse by peers or young people under the age of 18 is included, estimated prevalence rates of sexual abuse more than double.[76,77]

What do we know about juvenile sexual offenders? Approximately 70% have a history of sexual abuse, 65% have a history of physical abuse, 75% were neglected, 50% witnessed domestic violence, and 25% experienced all four types of maltreatment.[72] Although there is support for the use of clinic-based cognitive behavioral therapeutic interventions with juvenile sexual offenders,[78] the treatment with the strongest empirical support for juvenile sexual offenders is a variation of Multisystemic Therapy (MST).[79–81] MST is the home-based intervention originally developed for the treatment of multiproblem families that we discussed in Chapter 3, which also was adapted to address the substance abuse treatment needs of parents involved with the child welfare system. As discussed previously, MST home-based interventions are individualized and flexible. They incorporate well-validated treatment strategies derived from family therapies, behavioral parent training, and cognitive-behavioral therapy, and are designed to address child (e.g., trauma history, psychiatric diagnoses), family (e.g., inconsistent discipline, low monitoring, family conflict), and extrafamilial (e.g., association with deviant peers, school difficulties) factors that are associated with youth antisocial behavior, including sexual offending. The three main adaptations made to MST for work with juvenile sexual offenders include a protocol to address denial about the abusive behavior; a protocol to address safety risk to potential victims; and protocols to promote age-appropriate and normative social experiences with peers.

In a randomized controlled trial of this adaptation of MST with 127 adjudicated juvenile sexual offenders, at 12-month follow-up, relative to youth who received treatment as usual, youth who received MST had significantly greater reductions in sexual behavior problems as rated by caregivers, youth, and review of official arrest records. They also had a greater reduction in delinquency, substance use, and fewer out-of-home placements. These gains were retained over a 2-year follow-up period, with a lower number of arrests also reported for the MST group. Arrests were predominantly for nonsexual offenses; there were only four sexual offense arrests from baseline to the 2-year follow-up.[79,80] (See the MST-Problem Sexual Behavior (PSB) treatment website for a list of licensed MST-PSB programs and contact information for training, http://www.mstpsb.com/Pages/default.aspx).

Trauma-Focused Cognitive Behavior Therapy (TF-CBT), the intervention with the strongest evidence base for the treatment of PTSD in children, also has been found to be effective in addressing problem sexual behavior in children with a history of sexual abuse. When compared with children who received nondirected supportive psychotherapy, children who received TF-CBT had significantly greater reduction in Child Sexual Behavior Inventory scores at the termination of treatment, with these gains showing ongoing improvement over a 1-year follow-up period.[82] There is also some preliminary evidence that Prolonged Exposure Therapy, another evidence-based treatment for PTSD, is effective at reducing inappropriate sexualized behaviors in juvenile offenders with chronic PTSD.[83]

Inappropriate sexualized behaviors in children and adolescents in the child welfare system are common and treatable.[73,74] Research suggests that juvenile sexual offenders have more in common with other conduct-disordered youth than with adult sex offenders. Data also suggest that risk of sexual recidivism for juveniles is relatively low; however, it is often difficult to predict risk on an individual basis. Nonetheless, available data suggest transferring juvenile offenders to adult criminal court actually increases the risk of recidivism. Developmentally appropriate treatment is the preferred course of action. (For a practical guide to the evaluation and treatment of juvenile sexual offenders, see Reference 73.)

When it comes to problem sexual behavior in the child welfare system, I advocate for a universal precautions approach. In medicine, universal precaution refers to avoiding contact with patients' bodily fluids, assuming all patients could be possible carriers of HIV or other blood-borne pathogens. By universal precautions within the child welfare system, I propose assuming all children entering the system may display inappropriate sexualized behaviors. Problem sexualized behaviors are not always evident at time of initial placement and frequently emerge over time.[84] Children should not be labeled, but rather universally taught appropriate touching and interpersonal boundaries. Foster parents and other community providers should be taught safety procedures to minimize risk of child victimization, told how to respond if these behaviors occur, and familiarized with the types of services to seek if indicated. Again, because workers are the gatekeepers to accessing services, training of caseworkers is also essential.

Enough policy and research for now; let's get back to our story and see how Samya is faring at her new foster home.

8

Looking for a Home without a Dog that Bites
(399 DAYS IN OUT-OF-HOME CARE)

Samya is sitting by the fan watching TV when the doorbell rings. Her new foster mother calls out "coming" in a singsong voice as she waddles to the front door. The family's pug barks loudly and Samya cringes. She watches with a skeptical eye as her foster mother cheerfully greets Carly.

Samya stays on the couch facing the TV, but her attention is on the exchange between her new foster mother and her worker. After a few minutes, Carly invites Samya to join the two of them in the kitchen.

There is a plate of cookies on the kitchen table. Samya thinks about taking one but decides not to. Samya sits on the far side of the table and looks down at the ground. Her foster mother is complaining about the heat and chatting on about how she cannot wait to leave for their vacation at the Cape the following week.

She asks Carly, "Have you arranged respite care for Samya yet?"

"There's a foster family in the next town over that agreed to keep Samya while you're away. I'll be able to pick her up next Friday afternoon, and she can stay with them while you are off on vacation."

Samya thinks about her trip to Virginia Beach with the Olsens. She misses living with them, and thinks she would not want to go to the Cape with her new foster mother even if she were invited.

When there is a break in the conversation, Samya looks up at Carly and asks, "Have you seen my mom? How's she doin? When will I get to see her again?"

Carly's tone of voice changes, and somehow as she talks, Samya feels as though she is in trouble, like she has done something wrong.

"Your mom's okay, but she's not doing what she's supposed to be doing. The judge is giving her another chance to show him she's ready to take care of you, but you won't be going home any time soon, and there are no plans for visits with your mom to resume until she makes progress with the court orders."

Carly hopes her response will suffice and end the discussion about Samya's mother. She does not want to tell Samya about her supervisor's two phone calls with Samya's mother. She does not want Samya to know that Maria is staying at a battered women's shelter, that her last boyfriend beat her with a crowbar, that she was treated in the ER for double vision after being hit in the head, or that she has been on crutches because she tore some ligaments in her leg after tripping while trying to run away from her boyfriend.

Samya's worker and foster mother resume chatting about things, but Samya loses track of what they are saying. She is lost in her own thoughts. After about 15 minutes, Carly asks Samya to walk her out to her car.

The two walk silently out of the kitchen, across the living room, and down the front steps. When they get to the driveway, Carly turns around and faces Samya.

"I got a call from your therapist. She let me know you are worried about your foster mother's niece."

Samya recounts the incident when the little four-year-old visited and how she was taken to another room after misbehaving. Samya says she heard slaps and cries, and saw a red hand print on the girl's little cheek when she came back out to the kitchen.

"I asked her what happened and she said my foster mom hit her."

"We are going to investigate."

Samya looks up at Carly and says, "I really don't feel safe here."

Then, trying to ignore the lump in the back of her throat, Samya looks down and stops speaking for a few seconds. She then goes on to say in a less serious, almost playful tone, "Do you know that dog has bit me three times?"

She shows Carly several dog bite marks on her thigh and states with an air of determination, "I really don't want to stay in this home."

Carly says she will talk with her supervisor and see what can be done. She reviews safety plans with Samya, gives her a hug, then gets in her car and drives away. Samya stays on the driveway long after the taillights are gone, surprised by the chill she feels in the midst of the summer heat wave. Knowing that Shannon will be by in a bit to pick her up for a visit with her brother eases her mind.

On the ride to Sylar's foster home, Samya complains to Shannon about her foster mom and the dog. She is upbeat when she gets to Sylar's home, and it is a good visit filled with basketball, videogames, and light-hearted conversation. As they prepare to leave, Shannon reminds Sylar she will be picking him up the next morning for their sibling therapy session. Sylar then gives Samya a hug before she gets in the car.

The next morning Sylar looks impatiently out the window of the Child Guidance Center, because it is after nine o'clock and Samya is late for their appointment. Within a few minutes he sees her walking toward the clinic door with her new foster mother, whom Sylar has not met yet. His sister is wearing shorts and a tank top.

All of a sudden, after opening the exterior door of the clinic and walking into the vestibule, Samya falls to her knees, bangs her head against the wall, and crumbles to the floor. Samya's foster mother stops walking and looks down at Samya.

Sylar and Shannon rush to the foyer. Sylar carefully picks Samya up and carries her into the waiting room. He sits on the ground holding Samya. Her thin frail arms are limp, her eyes are closed, and the bronze luster is drained from her face.

"Samya. Samya."

Sylar and Shannon both repeatedly call out Samya's name, and Shannon gently slaps Samya's face trying to revive her. Samya's foster mother stands a few feet back.

Samya's eyes roll back in her head. She mumbles some incomprehensible words, but then is unresponsive. Shannon runs to get a wet paper towel and ask the person at the front desk to call 9-1-1.

When Shannon comes back, Samya's therapist is also in the waiting room. She asks Samya's foster mother what is going on.

In a slightly annoyed tone of voice she says, "I have no idea what she's doing. We were running late this morning. I got her up. We didn't have time for breakfast. We got in the car and we came here."

Samya rolls over and grabs her side. She brings her knees to her chest and moans. Sylar gently rubs her back.

Within minutes two paramedics approach and begin firing questions, first at Samya's foster mother, then at anyone who will answer. Shannon let them know that Samya has a history of seizures, problems with anxiety, and had not eaten that morning.

One of the paramedics checks Samya's vitals, and together they put her on a stretcher. "Will you be riding with her in the ambulance?" one of the paramedics asks her foster mother.

"No. I want to have my own car. I'll meet you at the hospital."

Sylar walks alongside the stretcher as the paramedics roll Samya out the clinic doors. He stands immobilized on the street until the ambulance is out of sight. Sylar's eyes then begin to water. When Shannon notices his tears she says she will call Carly to see if it is okay for her to drive him to the hospital so he can be with his sister.

Once back inside the clinic, Sylar goes to the restroom. Shannon then asks Samya's therapist, "Is it just my imagination, or did Samya's foster mother not seem the least bit concerned about any of this?"

"She seemed as if it was an imposition, not an emergency."

Shannon then calls Carly and gets permission from the social work supervisor to take Sylar to the hospital to check up on Samya.

When Sylar and Shannon arrive at the hospital, Samya's foster mother is sitting in the waiting room alone. Samya is off by herself having some tests.

After what seems like an eternity, a nurse comes to let them know they can go back and see Samya.

Samya is propped up on several pillows and the color has returned to her face. Her big brown eyes sparkle as Sylar and Shannon walk in the room. She seems back to herself—complaining that the wooden board hurt her back, and saying that she cannot believe they haven't fed her anything yet. She is starving.

Sylar, Shannon, and Samya chat brightly about miscellaneous nothings to help pass the time. Samya's foster mother rests in the corner and does not contribute much to the conversation. By noon, Sylar and Shannon say their goodbyes.

A bit before four o'clock, the doctor from the hospital calls Carly to give her an update. Although he originally thought Samya passed out because she had not eaten, after being fed she developed lower abdominal pain, a fever, and began vomiting. He says he now thinks she has appendicitis and is planning to do a CT scan with contrast to verify the diagnosis. If it is appendicitis, he will need permission to treat papers faxed immediately. Carly says she will take care of this, and asks to speak to Samya.

"How are you?"

"Miserable. I never made it to my therapy session today. I passed out on the way in and hit my head. I am not sure which hurts more, my stomach or my head."

"You know the doctor is thinking you may have appendicitis? He is going to do one more test, and if it is positive, you are going to need surgery."

"I know. I'm kinda scared. I never had surgery before."

"I'll ask your foster mom to go back to the hospital. She'll be with you for the surgery and I'll be by to see you tomorrow."

"Does my mom know I'm in the hospital? Can I see her?"

"I'll call your mom and let her know. I'll try to bring her for a visit tomorrow."

By 7:30 Samya is in surgery. Her foster mother is by her side when they come to take her down to the operating room. Samya cannot help but wish it were her real mom instead. The night passes in a blur. She wakes up once as a nurse is taking her vitals, and cries gently as she falls back to sleep.

The next afternoon Carly arrives—with Samya's *mother!* She has not seen her mother for two months, since visits were suspended.

One of her last conversations with Carly about the judge's decision to suspend visits replays in her head. "Your mother has things she has to do to show she wants you and Sylar to come home. She's not doing them."

Samya and her mother embrace with broad smiles and tears welling in their eyes. Samya then pulls away and asks, "When are you going to do what you gotta do so I can come home?"

"Oh baby, you know I'm trying. I am staying at My Daughter's Shelter now. I left Ken cuz he almost killed me. Beat me up with a crow bar the night I …"

Carly interrupts, but not quite soon enough.

"That's not appropriate conversation."

Samya's mind drifts off for a minute. Hearing her mom say she was at a shelter makes her think of all the shelters where she and Sylar stayed with their mom. The year before DCF took them there must have been three or four of these. Her mom's chatter brings her back to the present.

"I am sorry baby. How are you doing? How do you like your new foster home?"

"I hate it. I've been bit three times by the dog. See, you can still see where he bit me last. And I don't feel safe there. Last weekend my foster mom's niece was at the house. She was being kinda bad so my foster mom took her into the laundry room for a talkin', but it sounded like there was more than just talkin' going on. The little girl came out crying with a red mark on her cheek. I asked if she was hit, and she said yeah."

"What kinda place do you have my daughter at?"

"Samya and I have talked about these things. We are looking into it."

The conversation shifts to reminiscing about old times. Samya then turns on the radio and asks her mom to sit next to her on the bed. They seem more like sisters than mother and daughter, singing one song after another and chatting like teens.

The hour is up in a flash, and it is time to say goodbye. When Samya is left alone in the hospital room, she focuses her attention on the talk show on the TV and tries not to pay attention to the sad feeling in her gut.

Later that day Samya's foster mother calls Carly. She lets her know that she does not want Samya to return to her home. She says she is angry about the allegations involving the incident with her niece, and she hangs up the phone before Carly has any time to comment.

Carly then calls over to the hospital and speaks to Samya.

"How are you feeling?"

"A lot better. The doctor says I am ready to leave the hospital."

"I may be by to pick you up later today, but it may not be until tomorrow. You are going to go to a new foster home."

"Where?"

"I don't know yet."

"Well, that's a little scary. Can you try to find me a home without a dog that bites?"

"I'll do the best I can."

In the two days following Samya's discharge from the hospital, not only does she have to meet a new foster mother; but her case is transferred to a new social worker yet again—Monica (DCF-W7).

Allegations of Abuse in Foster Care

Although federal legislation sets minimum standards of definitions of child abuse and neglect for states that accept federal funding, each state is responsible for defining child maltreatment in state law. There is no uniform definition of physical abuse, or any other form of maltreatment in the United States. In some states, threatening harm and acts such as striking a child in the face or on the head constitute physical abuse. Most states, however, require evidence of harm through nonaccidental physical injury, and a few states detail the nature of the injuries that are needed to indicate physical abuse (e.g., substantial or multiple skin bruising, soft tissue swelling, internal bleeding, bone fracture, burns).[85] Although nonaccidental injury of children according to the various state-specific definitions is unlawful, corporal punishment is allowed in the home of birth families in every state. It is not allowed in most out-of-home placement settings, however. As of June 2014, 40 states prohibited the use of corporal punishment in foster homes or institutions, with Connecticut being among the states that forbids use of physical discipline in foster care placements.[86]

It is estimated that each year there are allegations of child maltreatment filed involving close to 10% of the population of children living in foster care.[87] The majority of these allegations—80%–90%—are *not* verified,[87] with federal data suggesting, in a given year that 2% or fewer of all children in foster care are victims of a substantiated maltreatment report involving a foster parent.[11]

Official substantiated rates of child maltreatment, however, are likely an underestimation. Based on adolescent self-report, rates of physical abuse are suggested to be significantly elevated in both foster care and residential care settings compared with population estimates, and several-fold greater than official substantiated rates suggest.[88] Self-report data from adolescents in care suggest rates of sexual abuse are no greater in foster care than in the general public, but they are more than double the population rate among youth living in group care settings.[89]

It is estimated that 5% of placement disruptions are due to abuse allegations.[61] Although 80%–90% of abuse allegations are not verified, a subset are likely not verified due to biases inherent in having state-run child welfare agencies investigate state-operated foster homes and institutions. Others may not be verified because of insufficient evidence, and a subset may indeed represent false allegations, although there is no way to know what proportion of allegations is indeed fabricated.

False allegations can be very stressful for foster parents to experience, and some excellent resources have been developed to help foster parents in such circumstances.[90,91] Why would a foster child allege something that is not true? Sometimes children who have been abused are highly sensitive to triggers that they associate with past incidents of abuse. Yelling, or the touch of a hand on their shoulders, can trigger flashbacks and distort the experience of what is happening in the here and now with memories of what happened in the past. Also as children age through the foster care system, they learn that allegations are a ticket out of a placement, as well as a way to keep foster parents who are starting to get too close a safe distance away.[92] (See References 90 and 91 for further information.)

I do not know whether the allegations against Samya's foster mother were substantiated, or whether she lost her foster care license. I do know, however, that Samya never saw her former foster mother again, and after she was placed in her new foster home, she never saw Carly again.

Let's resume the story so we can see what happens next for Samya.

9

An Inch from Death

(448 DAYS IN OUT-OF-HOME CARE)

As Shannon pulls into the driveway she sees Samya sitting on the front steps. Her hair is neatly styled and she is wearing a coral sundress. There are two Kohl's shopping bags by her side. When Samya sees Shannon's car, she pops up, opens the door to the house to call goodbye to her new foster mother, Tori, and then bounds down the stairs and into the front seat of the car.

"Why are you so dressed up today?"

"I wanted to show Sylar this new dress and all the stuff Tori got me for school."

"Things still going well at Tori's house?"

"I want to stay there forever."

"You've only been there about a month. Wait and see what happens." As Shannon says this she is thinking about how excited Samya was when she first moved to the last foster home; she is worried things may change and she does not want Samya to be more disappointed than necessary.

Sylar is outside waiting for Samya when she arrives at his foster home. He gives her a hug when she gets out of the car, and the two start chatting immediately. The visit is off to a better start than the last one, in which Sylar was uncommunicative and sullen the entire hour. They all go into the house, and Samya shows Sylar her new stuff while they sit at the dining room table.

"You are so lucky you get to wear whatever you want to school. I have to wear a uniform."

"At least you know what you are going to wear each day. You don't have to waste any time picking out an outfit."

"All we get to choose is our shoes."

At this point one of the other foster boys in the home joins them at the table. The two boys start to argue about whose new sneakers are cooler. They run upstairs, grab their new sneakers, and ask Shannon and Samya to vote. "Which are cooler?" All three kids then settle in and play a noisy and rowdy game of Monopoly.

Three days after the sibling visit, Samya has another health scare, but she is sent home cleared after being evaluated at the ER for abdominal pain.

The following day Monica (DCF-W7), whom Samya met with twice since moving to the new foster home, telephones Tori to see how Samya is doing. She calls Tori at work, and Tori tells her Samya is doing well. Samya is actually with Tori, helping her fold clothes at the store. Monica asks to speak with Samya.

"I am glad you are feeling better. Shannon said you wanted to talk with me."

"Yes. I really want to be adopted by Tori."

The day before when Tori had called Monica to discuss school registration, she mentioned Samya indicated on two occasions that she wanted Tori to adopt her. Tori had said she had an interest in possibly adopting Samya, but she could not take Sylar. Monica said she would keep this interest in mind, and talk with her supervisor about it.

While talking on the telephone with Monica, Samya goes on to say, "I have been thinking about it since last week and I've talked to Tori about it. I don't want to go to another foster home. Tori spoils me and I really like being here."

"We can talk more about this on our drive to therapy on Tuesday."

On the drive to therapy a few days later, Samya reiterates that she wants to be adopted. She adds, "I don't want to go back to my mom anymore. The same old stuff is going to continue to happen and she's going to keep on using drugs."

Soon after this conversation, Samya joins a therapy group for kids whose parents' rights are apt to be terminated, freeing them up for adoption.

The honeymoon at Tori's house does not last, however. Within weeks of discussing her desire to be adopted, things start to unravel. Tori complains to Monica that Samya is sneaky at times; sneaking food and candy, and trying to sneak out to see boys. Conflict also erupts between Samya and her foster siblings. There are five foster children in the home, including Samya, and someone is always getting in someone else's stuff. The younger children frequently get on her nerves, but things are especially bad with Dahlia who is her same age. Dahlia and Samya are in competing cliques at school, and Dahlia reportedly shared confidential information about Samya's family with some of the other kids at school.

The family gossip at school makes Samya acutely suicidal and bombards her with thoughts like, "My own mother doesn't want me." The word "abandoned" replays again and again in her head. Tori is able to bring Samya back from this darkness.

A few weeks after Dahlia shared confidential information about Samya's family with some of the other kids at school, there is another incident that starts to further unravel Samya. She is at a party at Tori's niece's house and sees Joseph, who still has his waist-length dreadlocks. She has a panic attack and is flooded by a lot of horrific memories. Tori does not really understand who

Joseph is—but she is able to soothe Samya initially. When Tori mentions the incident to Monica—Monica does not know who Joseph is either—she does not know he is the man Maria was living with when Samya entered care. She also does not know Joseph put a belt around Maria's neck and nearly killed her more than once. It is too much for Samya to explain these things to Tori and Monica, so Samya keeps these memories to herself.

A week after Samya got distressed after running into Joseph, Monica again calls Tori to check in. Tori reports that Samya is doing better; she, in fact, is doing well. Samya has friends who call her at the house, and although she and Dahlia are still not getting along, there have been no major outbursts of late. She also reports that Samya has started calling her "Ma."

"Are you okay with her calling you 'Ma'?"

"I don't mind so long as Samya is comfortable with it."

Over the next few weeks, however, Samya starts having problems again. At 6:30 one night, Tori calls and catches Monica still in her office.

"I'm so glad I got you on the phone. Things have been deteriorating with Samya. I am not sure I can put up with it."

"What's been happening?"

"In addition to her interim report card showing she is failing four courses, she is continuing to be sneaky and she's started to lie. She didn't come home from school today and went to a friend's house without my permission. I took away her TV and radio privileges and she's all hissy. I can't deal with her."

"Would you like me to try to speak with her?"

"Please."

Tori hands the phone to Samya, who is sitting at the kitchen table, readily in earshot of all that was spoken.

"Hey."

"Hey."

"What happened today?"

"I just wanted to visit a friend and get out of the house. I sometimes feel like a prisoner here. I lost my TV and radio privileges today, and I'm not even allowed to use the phone to call my friends." Samya's voice cracks as she talks, as though she is fighting back tears.

"You lost your phone privileges because of your grades. Also, you can't just do whatever you want. You will have more privileges if you get your grades up and show better listening."

"I don't want to be here, and I don't know what I am going to do to myself if you don't get me out of here."

"Threatening to hurt yourself is no way to cope with how you feel about getting in trouble. If you really feel like you are going to hurt yourself, I'll call 9-1-1, but sitting in a hospital is no joke."

"You just don't want me to leave here."

"No, I don't, because I know you like it there. The only time you don't like it there is when you get in trouble for something."

Monica and Samya talk for a while about Samya taking responsibility for her behavior and not doing things without permission. The conversation then drifts to Maria.

"I don't want to live with my ma because she's not going to change her ways, but I'd like to see her."

"Do you know why you are not seeing your mom now?"

"Not really."

"Because she's not doing what she's supposed to be doing. She needs to address her issues and stop making promises she's not going to keep."

Monica pauses and thinks about her almost biweekly telephone calls from Maria. Maria is always asking about the kids and talking about starting new treatment programs, but every time Monica checks, Maria has never made it to more than four or five sessions before being administratively discharged for missing appointments.

The telephone call ends with a discussion about Samya's visits with Sylar and plans to have Sylar come for one of her basketball games, and for Samya to go to his winter choir concert. Monica then speaks to Tori before hanging up the phone. She says if Samya threatens to hurt herself again and she is worried, she should call 9-1-1. Both agree they do not think this will be necessary; Samya seems calm. No problems are anticipated for the night.

Monica next sees Samya and Sylar the following week at their sibling therapy session. She has letters Maria wrote for the children, along with wicker baskets Maria has asked her to give them. Samya's basket is white and decorated with a flowered ribbon and has a multicolored shorts set, sparkle pens, a sketch pad, stickers, a locket, and a letter; Sylar's basket is plain and has a jumbo pencil, an X-Men card game, a computer printout of action figures, a ring, multicolored gel pens, a sketch pad, and a letter. The gift bags were barer when Maria dropped them off at the office, but Monica added more things to them so they would not look so sparse.

They read the letters together. Maria's letters to the children say she loves and misses them, and that she will see them soon. She goes on to say she is getting her life back on track. She has found a three-bedroom apartment, and she has plans to fix up each of their rooms for them. After reading the letters, Monica dispels any ambiguity created by the notes.

"You won't really be going home any time too soon. Your mom still is not in a mental health or substance abuse treatment program. She's not taking care of the things she needs to take care of so things will be stable if you go back."

"The letter makes me think maybe she'll do it this time, but I worry if I go back, things won't really change. DCF will end up taking us again, and I'll lose my spot at Tori's house."

The carrot of hope is confusing for Samya and opens up a barely closed raw wound. Samya writes a letter back to her mother in which she thanks her mom for the gifts, but goes on to say:

". . . . I am sitting here crying, because it hurts me to tell you the truth of what I think . . . You know I can't stand the fact that I can't even see my mother because they say she's not doing what she needs to do!!! Ma, you know you are smarter than this. You are way smarter than this. Don't get me wrong, I will always love you and so will Sylar. . . but two years in DCF care is too long, Ma . . . ."

The baskets and the letters bring an additional whirlwind of memories crashing down on Samya. One night about a week after receiving the basket, she becomes overwhelmed by relentless images of a time her mother tried to commit suicide. Samya makes several superficial cuts on her wrist with a cuticle scissor to try to distract herself from the unending pictures in her head. Tori calls the DCF hotline, and the person on the other end instructs her to take Samya to the hospital for an evaluation.

"I won't be able to stay with her though, because I have to get to work."

The hotline worker arranges for an on-call staff to meet them at the hospital. A woman named Keisha from DCF is waiting in the ER when they arrive. Samya has never met Keisha before.

Tori is frazzled and asks to speak to Keisha in private. They cross over to the other side of the waiting room.

She confides, "You are going to have to find another place for Samya to go tonight if they discharge her. This is too much for me."

Keisha is able to convince Tori to change her mind. As Tori leaves the hospital she states in a voice loud enough for Samya to hear, "Okay, she can come back to my home, but this will be her last chance."

Samya is sent home from the hospital that night, although the pictures in her head and the urge to hurt herself are not completely gone. Keisha gives Samya her number and says she can call if she ever wants to vent, but Samya never sees or speaks to Keisha again.

Two days later Monica gets a midday telephone call from Tori.

"The school just called. Samya and Dahlia got in a fight at school."

Tori sounds pretty exasperated, so Monica decides to try to stop by the house at the end of the day.

Monica gets to the house a bit before dinner. She pulls Samya aside and Samya lets her know she did not actually get in a fight with Dahlia at school. It was one of her friends who almost got in a fight with Dahlia, but a teacher broke things up before they got started. Monica, Samya, Tori, and Dahlia then all meet together in the living room.

"I know you both want us to get along, but I hate that girl. She is such a phony. She has no mind of her own and just does whatever her friends say. She could have stopped her friend from getting in my face, but she's too much of a wuss to stand up to anybody."

Samya looks down at the ground and does not respond to Dahlia's accusations.

Then Tori says to Monica, "Family meetings are always like this. Dahlia does most of the talking and Samya rarely says anything."

While noting how intimidated Samya looks, Monica remarks, "Samya is just less confrontational about things than you are, Dahlia. Also, she really can't control her friends."

The meeting ends with a consensus that the girls do not have to like each other, but they need to be cordial and respectful of one another, given that they are foster sisters, live in the same house, and go to the same school.

Two weeks later, an exasperated Tori again calls Monica.

"I like Samya, but I am on the verge of asking for her to be removed. Here's everything that has happened in the past 24 hours: Samya told Tia, the four-year-old in my home, that she wants to kill herself; she threatened to punch Joli, the eight-year-old in my home; she stole Joli's headphones; and she put shaving cream in Dahlia's bed last night."

Twenty minutes later, Tori is again appeased, but Monica is not sure how many more rounds of this the placement can endure.

Over the next two weeks, the conflict in the home continues. Samya talks to her therapist about how she fantasizes about strangling Dahlia. She would not actually do it, but it makes her less angry to think these things. It is also a good distraction from the movies replaying in her head of scenes when she lived with her mother.

One afternoon in therapy, while Samya is talking about how her mom's ex-boyfriend David used to beat on everyone in the house, she tells her therapist she often thinks about putting a pillow over her head and slitting her own throat with a butcher knife. Her therapist decides to call an ambulance and have Samya evaluated at the ER again.

When the paramedics arrive and walk into the therapy room where Samya is waiting, Samya glances up with vacant eyes. They see a girl who has not combed her hair in days, sitting on the floor, hunched over, back against the wall. They assist her up and help her walk out of the clinic to the ambulance parked out on the street.

Samya is transported alone in the ambulance from the clinic to the hospital. A request was made for an on-call DCF worker to meet her at the ER, but one never arrives. This time Samya is admitted to the hospital.

In describing how she feels to the ER doc, she says, "I am tired all the time. I feel like I am an inch from death."

Samya never returns to Tori's home, and Tori has no contact with Samya while she is in the psychiatric hospital over the next three months. Dreams of being adopted fade into the distant past and are replaced with flashbacks and the harsh reality that she is essentially alone.

Child Abuse and Risk for Psychiatric and Medical Health Problems

As part of our research, we completed a follow-up evaluation with Samya one week before her removal from the Olsen's home. This was two months before she was referred to the psychiatrist affiliated with the Safe Home and first diagnosed with major depression. Samya was not depressed then. At that time, she received a score of four on a standardized scale of depression—well below the threshold of clinical significance. She also completed a social network questionnaire at that time. Samya was asked to name people she (1) talked to about personal things; (2) counted on to buy the things she needed; (3) shared good news with; (4) got together with to have fun; and (5) went to if she needed advice. She listed Mrs. Olsen in response to each of these probes—and Mrs. Olsen was listed as her top support—the person she counted on most. Her brother, Mr. Olsen, and Maria were also named on her list of supports, but Mrs. Olsen was her number one go-to person despite experiencing mixed loyalties and conflicting feelings toward the two "mothers" in her life.

The availability of a caring and stable parent or alternate guardian is one of the most important factors in promoting resiliency in maltreated children. In our own research, the presence of positive social supports has been found to ameliorate risk for depression associated with a history of abuse,[93] as well as risk for depression associated with genetic factors.[94,95] Depression, like most psychiatric and medical health problems, is caused by a combination of genetic and environmental factors, but the effects of these factors are not fixed or predetermined.

Caspi and colleagues were the first to show that the serotonin transporter (SERT) gene moderates risk for depression in adults with a history of child maltreatment.[96] The SERT gene makes a transporter that is located on the outer edge of brain cells and is responsible for bringing serotonin back into the cell so it can be reutilized; this is also the site of action of antidepressant drugs like Prozac. There are two common forms of the SERT gene, one designated "s" because it is shorter than the other version, the other labeled "l" because it is the longer of the two. Because everyone has two copies of every gene and receives one copy from their mother, and the other copy from their father, there are three common SERT genotypes: ll, ls, and ss, with the ss genotype considered highest risk. Caspi and colleagues found that individuals with a history of child abuse with the low-risk ll genotype were at no greater risk for depression than individuals without a history of abuse as children, but those with a history of abuse and the high-risk ss genotype were twice as likely to have an episode of depression during their lifetime. Individuals with the ss genotype who did not have a history of abuse were at no greater risk for depression than individuals with the ll genotype, so it appears the ss genotype only increases risk for depression in those individuals with a history of significant lifetime stress.

We observed a similar finding in children,[95] and because depression is not caused by just one gene, we also examined the effect of the brain-derived neurotrophic factor (BDNF) gene. This gene is important for brain development, underlies the action of many antidepressant drugs, and also has been implicated in the etiology of depression.[94] The maltreated children with the ss high-risk SERT genotype reported more depressive symptoms than the other maltreated children, and the maltreated children who had both the high risk SERT gene and the high-risk form of the BDNF gene reported the most symptoms of depression. The finding that the SERT genotype can modify risk for depression in individuals with a history of child maltreatment,[97] and that the BDNF genotype can further exacerbate this vulnerability,[98] has been replicated by numerous other investigators.

But as alluded to at the opening of this section, the availability of a loving and stable caregiver has been found to reduce risk for depression among maltreated children—even among those children with the highest genetic vulnerability for depression.[94] The maltreated children in our studies who could identify an adult in their lives that they lived with or saw regularly, on whom they could count for all the things children need, reported very few depressive symptoms. This was true even among the maltreated children with the high-risk SERT and the high-risk BDNF genes. The availability of a positive supportive caregiver alleviated the risk for depression in these children.

How can experiences in the environment—negative ones like child abuse and neglect, or positive ones like having a stable loving caregiver—alter the impact of high-risk genes on child outcomes? Much of what we know about the effects of experience on brain, behavior, and genes comes from animal research, with studies by Michael Meaney and colleagues the first to start to unravel how variation in early life experiences can affect stress reactivity and risk for depression, anxiety, and other health problems later in life.[99,100]

Meaney and colleagues developed a rat model of early neglect by studying ideal and nonoptimal or "neglectful" rat moms. Defining "neglectful" behavior in rats is a bit easier than defining it in humans. Ideal rat moms lick and groom their offspring practically nonstop, providing continuous tactile stimulation to their young. Neglectful rat moms are "low-lickers and groomers"—they provide minimal tactile stimulation to their rat pups. Meaney and colleagues identified consistent differences in the offspring of high- and low-licking and grooming moms, abbreviated as high-LG and low-LG moms.

Before discussing their findings, it will be helpful to provide a brief review of the stress response. The brain responds to stress in an orchestrated manner, with the regions of the brain that are responsible for responding to stress overlapping with many of the parts of the brain that work together to regulate moods and behavior. The stress response and the impact of early adversity on brain development are detailed elsewhere and will not be elaborated upon in this text.[101–105] There is one cascade within the stress response, however, that is worth discussing in some detail, because work on this aspect of the stress response has laid the groundwork for understanding how early experience can alter gene expression and risk for negative outcomes following neglect and other forms of adversity.

Briefly, the stress response is turned on by the release of one hormone from the hypothalamus, which causes the release of another hormone from the pituitary, which then causes the release of glucocorticoids from the adrenals. In rats, corticosterone is the glucocorticoid released from the adrenals, in humans it is cortisol. What is important to remember about this chemical cascade is that glucocorticoids feedback on the system to shut off the stress response. Glucocorticoids feedback on the hypothalamus to turn off the stress response, and they also feedback on one other brain structure as well—the hippocampus. The hippocampus is especially critical for putting the brakes on the stress response, and work by Meaney and colleagues shows that the ability of the hippocampus to put the brakes on the stress response is affected by variation in early maternal care.[101]

Meaney and colleagues have found that when compared to offspring of low-LG (neglectful) moms, offspring of high-LG (optimal) moms have significantly more glucocorticoid receptors in the hippocampus—that brain part that is key in putting the brakes on the stress response. Consequently, offspring of high LG-moms exhibit low stress reactivity as adult animals, are relatively fearless in novel situations, and show great resilience when faced with challenges. In contrast, offspring of low-LG rat moms have fewer glucocorticoid receptors in the hippocampus and a heightened stress response. They also are more likely to freeze or get quite agitated and anxious in new environments, and give up easily when faced with hardships, with the tendency for rats to give up when challenged in various experimental paradigms considered an analogue for depressive behavior in humans.

How do we know these individual differences are due to variation in maternal care and not due to prenatal intrauterine or genetic factors? In rats, one can perform experimental manipulations that one cannot perform in children. Meaney and colleagues did cross-fostering studies in which they had high-LG moms raise the offspring of low-LG moms from immediately after birth, and low-LG moms raise the offspring of high-LG moms. As adults the rat pups had characteristics one would predict based on the parenting style of their "foster" mothers, not the characteristics of their birth mothers. Emerging data growing from this body of work suggests that variation in early child rearing experiences is key to programming the stress response and conferring risk for anxious and depression-like behaviors.

So how does an individual difference in maternal behavior translate into modifications in glucocorticoid receptor number and alterations in stress reactivity and vulnerability to psychopathology? Meaney and colleagues found changes in glucocorticoid receptor number are mediated by epigenetic mechanisms.[100,106–108] Epigenetics refers to chemical modifications to genes that do not involve mutations or a change in DNA base pairs.[100] These chemical modifications can alter gene activity and play a role in acute regulation of genes in response to changes in the environment.[109,110] In particular, the addition of a methyl-group—one carbon atom and three hydrogen atoms—changes the three-dimensional shape of the DNA and the likelihood of a given gene product being made, which in this case is the likelihood of glucocorticoid receptors being made in the hippocampus. With fewer of these receptors, the offspring of low-LG animals are less able to turn off the stress response; they secrete more stress hormones, and display more anxiety- and depression-like behaviors.

It appears these epigenetic mechanisms, may not only increase risk for stress-related psychiatric and substance use disorders, but for a whole host of medical health problems as well. Numerous studies have shown that a history of child abuse and other adverse early experiences predicts a broad range of medical problems, including ischemic heart disease, stroke, diabetes, and cancer, in addition to mental health and substance use disorders.[111,112] The emerging data from our group suggests risk for this broad range of health problems also may be mediated by epigenetic mechanisms—chemical changes to the DNA that do not involve a mutation or change in DNA base pairs.[107] Although epigenetic changes are frequently long lasting, they need not be permanent, and can be altered at various points in development by subsequent experience.[113]

Although our understanding of gene regulation and epigenetics is in its infancy, this growing body of research offers significant promise in understanding risk and promoting resiliency in maltreated children.[113–115] Animal studies are helping us to understand better the effects of early stress on gene regulation and brain development, and delineate sensitive periods of development—times in development when individuals are more sensitive to both the positive and negative influences in the environment. In addition, animal studies are starting to delineate ways to expand the windows of sensitivity to reverse the effects of early adversity.[116]

The important take-home messages from this brief treatise are (1) child maltreatment need not lead to bad outcomes; (2) genetic effects are not fixed and can be modified by the environment; and (3) the availability of positive stable attachment figures is one of the most important factors in promoting resiliency in maltreated children.

For further discussion on these topics see References 99–105; 108–110; and 114–116. For now, let's return to our story and get caught up on what is happening with Sylar.

10

Without a Family

(571 DAYS IN OUT-OF-HOME CARE)

Sylar feels as though he is on the set of *CSI: Crime Scene Investigations*, except, this is no TV show being shot. This is his life. He is at the Derby police station. Monica is in the corner of the room, eyes on him, and he is sitting at a metal table across from two cops.

"Your foster mother said there will be no Christmas for you or any of the boys in the house if you don't return the jewelry that you took from her."

"I did not take her jewelry. They checked my locker at school today and it wasn't there."

"So why does she think you took it?"

"When I first moved in her home I stole a watch from her, but I returned it. I did not take this other stuff that's missing."

Sylar and the two detectives go in circles about the missing jewelry for about 20 minutes. One of the detectives then stands up and suggests that Monica take Sylar home and let his foster mother know that they do not think he took the jewelry.

As Sylar and Monica walk out of the two-story red-brick police station, the snow on the ground makes it look like Christmas, but there is not much else that makes it feel like Christmas.

Sylar turns to Monica and says, "I am tired of getting blamed for stuff I did not do just because I messed up in the past."

"After the holidays, I will see what other placement options there are for you."

As Monica says this, she thinks about her conversation with Marla's adult daughter, who is responsible for watching the boys while Marla is at work in the afternoons. A few months back she called to complain that Sylar's room was a pigsty, and that he was stealing candy in the middle of the night and leaving wrappers in his bed. When Monica talked to Sylar about these complaints, he asked, "If they have all these concerns about me, why do they keep me?" She remembered replying, "Because they like you and want to help you." When Monica conveyed this anecdote to Marla's daughter, she objected to the phrase "like him." She said, matter-of-factly, that she and her mother do not particularly like Sylar. She said, "Quite honestly, there's not a whole lot about him that's likeable—he's a pain in the ass—and we got eight boys in the home—all with issues."

On the car ride back to the foster home, Monica let Sylar know that Samya was hospitalized two days earlier. The hospital will be scheduling telephone calls and sibling therapy sessions. She says she plans on going to the sibling therapy sessions, too, but there probably will not be any until after the holiday.

When Monica picks Sylar up for the first sibling therapy session one week after New Year's Day, she asks, "How was your Christmas?"

Sylar replies, "OK. I played Dragon Balls Z video games most of the day."

"Did Marla ever find her jewelry?"

"It was at the bottom of one of the kid's closets. She got it all back."

When Monica and Sylar come onto the hospital psychiatric unit, Samya runs across the lobby to greet them. She gives them both a big hug. They are then escorted by Samya's psychiatrist, a petite Asian woman, into a private therapy room with a purple couch, several wooden chairs, and a dollhouse and chest of toys in the corner of the room.

There is an awkward silence when they first sit down. Dr. Li and Monica both look over at Samya who looks down at the floor.

Dr. Li then begins. She directs her gaze at Sylar. "Samya has just begun talking about something, something that she wants you to know about."

Sylar turns to look at Samya. She turns her head away, bites her lip, and fights back tears.

Dr. Li touches Samya on the leg to get her attention. Samya turns and looks at her.

"Do you want to tell Sylar what you told me about, or do you want me to tell him?"

In a barely audible voice, Samya says, "You."

Sylar turns to look at Dr. Li. He wishes he had sat on the couch next to his sister.

"When your sister was 10 years old and you still lived in New York, your sister was raped by your mom's friend Skip. It happened that night the two of you slept over at his house. Samya said Skip woke her up, brought her into his room, held his hand over her mouth, and raped her. Skip then made her take a shower and threatened to kill her if she told anyone. You slept through the incident."

"What's wrong with me that I didn't wake up?"

"It's not your fault. I don't blame you. I just wanted you to know."

Over time the conversation drifts to the situation with Tyrell when they were living with the Olsens.

Samya says, "I felt kinda betrayed by you. I know I agreed to things, and I did like Tyrell, but it felt a little like you sold me."

"I am sorry. I guess it was messed up."

Samya then lets the theme of the incident with Tyrell drop. She says, "You know I have spoken to the Olsens twice since I have been in the hospital."

"How are they?"

"Good. I might get to see them when I get out."

The session ends on a positive note. Monica takes Sylar back to his foster home and lets him know he has an interview with a new foster care agency in two weeks.

A few days after the sibling therapy session, Monica receives a phone call from Sylar's therapist.

"I wanted to let you know that I am going to call the child abuse hotline about Marla's daughter."

"How come?"

"Marla is the one who is the licensed foster care provider, but it is her daughter who is running the house. It seems to me that all the kids in the home have difficulty with her."

"What have you heard?"

"Sylar said that she is constantly yelling and screaming at the boys in the home, and breaks things when she's mad. She also reportedly has hit the boys, locked them out of the house when she's angry with them, and withheld food if they did not do their homework or some of their chores."

"Thanks for following up with this. I knew things weren't great there, but I did not know it was this bad."

"Sylar told me he has an interview with another foster care agency in a few weeks."

"Yes, the appointment is on the 23rd."

"He deserves better."

"I agree he does."

On the way over to the interview with the new foster care agency a few weeks later, Sylar let Monica know that he got a part in the school play.

"I didn't do this type of stuff when I was living with my mom. I used to stay home from school to protect her. I have been able to do a lot more stuff since entering care." He pauses, and then adds, "My tastes are different now."

The interview lasts about an hour. When they get back in the car, Monica says the interview went well, but there are no openings in the new foster care agency just yet.

"I know it is hard to wait, but stay positive. A spot will open up."

Two weeks after Sylar's interview, there is another sibling therapy session at the hospital. Monica picks Sylar up for the appointment. When he gets in the car, he asks, "Have you heard anything from the new foster care agency yet?"

"No openings yet. How are you doing?"

"I'm OK."

"Are you? Your school social worker called last week and said you were flipping out, talking about Skip."

"It upsets me when I think about what he did to Samya, and it bothers me that I didn't do anything to stop it."

"You did not know it was happening. He tried to make sure of that."

When they get to the hospital, Samya again greets them both with big hugs. Dr. Li again joins them for the sibling therapy session in the room with the purple couch, but Monica starts the session this time.

"There's an upcoming court hearing to review your family's case with DCF. Up until now we've been recommending reunification, but at this point, we no longer think that is appropriate or feasible."

Monica pauses to look at Sylar and Samya who are sitting side-by-side on the couch, but neither of them says anything.

Monica then continues, "Your mom had a lot of things she needed to do to show us she's ready to take care of you, and she has not made much progress. She has secured housing, but she's still not in mental health or substance abuse treatment, and she's still testing positive for cocaine."

Sylar says, "I can't believe it's been almost two years, and she's only done one of the things she is supposed to do."

Samya turns and looks at her brother and says, "Yeah, I know."

Samya then turns and asks Monica, "Do you know if our mom is living with a man?"

"I don't think so."

"Well, that's good." She then asks, "Can we see our mom one last time? I haven't seen her since I was in the hospital for my appendicitis."

"Probably, I should be able to arrange that."

Sylar then looks at Monica and states, "No offense, but while things were pretty awful when we were with our mother, sometimes I am not so sure things are that much better now with us in foster care without a family." Sylar's voice cracks as he finishes this last statement.

Samya puts her hand on Sylar's arm and says, "Hey." She pauses to look at him, then adds, "I am your family; I'll always be your family."

"I know, but we only get to see each other an hour a week, and some weeks not at all."

Sylar then stands up, walks toward the door, and turns his back to everyone in the room. He rubs his eyes and focuses his attention on staying in control.

"We are working to try to find you a better place."

"I know," he says as he turns around. "It's just been hard with all the place-ments I've had since you guys took us from our mom. I can't help it, but more times than not, I just feel like I am completely alone and I have no family. Seeing my sister for a few hours a month is not enough."

Sylar sits back down. He is able to tuck these feelings away by the end of the session. Sylar and Samya go for a meal at the hospital café, and they joke with one another, keep the conversation light, and nothing more is said about foster care and family.

The feelings of sadness and being alone without family continue, however, just below the surface.

It is a week or two later. Sylar sits in his school social worker's office, in a chair across from her desk, with a blank stare on his face. He says to her, "I had a dream that I was dead last night. It felt peaceful."

"Have you actually been thinking about killing yourself?"

In a calm and monotone voice, he replies, "All the time."

"If you had to rate your desire to actually die on a scale from 1 to 10, with 1 meaning you have these thoughts but would never kill yourself, and 10 meaning you really want to die, what would you rate your desire to actually die?"

"A 10."

"And have you actually thought of how you might kill yourself?"

"I'd take a knife from the kitchen in Marla's house and cut my throat."

While Sylar sits in her office, the school social worker calls Monica and Sylar's outpatient therapist, Dr. Worth. Everyone agrees he should be brought to the emergency room for an evaluation.

Sylar is admitted to the psychiatric hospital later that day. He is started on an antidepressant and is discharged from the hospital the following week.

Over the next three weeks, Dr. Worth notes that Sylar goes from looking the happiest he has ever seen him in all the time he has worked with him, to blatantly manic and psychotic. Sylar is not sleeping. He believes he was bitten by a bat and is turning into a vampire, and he reports feeling angry 98% of the time. In addition, he is obsessed with thoughts about hurting Joseph because of what he did to his mother. Dr. Worth considers bringing Sylar to the hospital for an evaluation, but when he talks to Marla she says she does not think it is necessary and that Sylar's behavior around the house is the best it has ever been.

After a sibling visit the next day, things turn sour. The sibling visit takes place at the treatment center Safe Home where Samya was living again after she was discharged from the hospital. When the aide gets Sylar to his foster home after the visit, Sylar refuses to go inside the house. He starts walking down the driveway. The aide walks by Sylar's side. Sylar is breathing fast, and moving his arms in an agitated manner while he paces back and forth.

Sylar says in a muddled voice, "I know where Joseph lives. I am going to make him pay for what he did to my mom."

The aide replies, "You can't walk there from here."

"I have money. I can take a bus to Meriden."

"Not tonight."

The aide persuades Sylar to get back in the car and convinces him to go with him to the hospital for an evaluation. All the necessary approvals are obtained.

Sylar is again admitted to the hospital, where he is diagnosed with Bipolar Disorder. He never sees Marla, or her daughter, again. He lived with Marla just a little over a year.

After being on the hospital psychiatric unit one week and stabilized on Lithium, Sylar is approved for a visit to the new foster home that was identified for him through the agency he interviewed with a few weeks earlier. The agency cancels the visit, however, and states they are not comfortable having him go from the hospital to the foster home. They are worried that he might jeopardize the stability of the other children in the home. The foster care placement offer is rescinded.

Within three weeks of Sylar being admitted to the hospital, his doctor is pushing for discharge. He recommends a therapeutic foster or professional foster care placement, but none are available. He suggests that Sylar be discharged to a shelter while awaiting placement because he does not think it is good for him to just be biding his time on a locked unit.

When no foster homes can be identified, Monica starts submitting applications to residential treatment facilities. No openings are available in Connecticut. She finally finds a program with an opening in New York. Eight weeks after Sylar was admitted to the hospital, five weeks after he was cleared for discharge, and one day before Samya's birthday, Sylar is transported two hours to a residential treatment facility in upstate New York. Samya had requested a visit with Sylar for her birthday, but it will be a month before she sees him.

On the drive to the program in New York, Sylar is in a daze. He is riding along with yet another new worker. Before leaving the hospital, he and Samya were each assigned their own new caseworkers from the adolescent services unit: Lynn (DCF-W8) and Barry (DCF-W9).

Psychotropic Drug Use Among Youth in the Child Welfare System

In 2003, when Sylar was admitted to the hospital after becoming manic, there were two published reports about children in foster care and the use of psychotropic medications—drugs prescribed for psychiatric disorders. The first paper was published in 1999. The authors surveyed 302 foster parents of six- to twelve-year-old children who were in foster care a minimum of six months. The authors reported that 16% of the elementary-school-aged children were prescribed psychotropic medications.[117] The second paper was published in 2001. The authors analyzed computerized claims data for a sample of over 15,000 birth-to-19-year-old children with Medicaid insurance. The authors reported that 30% of the children and adolescents in the sample who were living in foster care were prescribed psychotropic medications, a rate nearly double the rate of psychotropic drug use among youth receiving supplemental security income (SSI) for diagnosed disabilities, and 15 times the rate of youngsters receiving other forms of aid, with most children in this latter category receiving welfare—Aid to Families with Dependent Children (AFDC).[118]

At the time Sylar was hospitalized for becoming manic, there were no systematic records kept of the medications foster children were prescribed. To locate this data for our research we had to hunt and peck through random case notes in the DCF file. Connecticut, however, was among the first states to organize children's medication information. By 2007, it was one of only three states, together with Illinois and Tennessee, to establish databases to monitor the use of psychotropic medications for children in state custody.[119]

By 2008 there were several other papers published on the topic of psychotropic drug use among children in foster care. One paper reported that 12% of birth-to-five-year-old children in foster care were prescribed psychiatric drugs,[120] and another study reported that 41% of the foster care children on psychotropic drugs were prescribed three or more different types of medications (e.g., stimulant, antidepressant, antipsychotic), with antipsychotic drugs used at very high rates.[121] This raised concern, because some antipsychotic drugs are associated with significant weight gain and other adverse medical side effects. Another paper published about the same time, with a cohort of youth aging out of the system, reported similar rates of psychotropic drug use to previous studies, but also noted that 41% of the adolescents diagnosed with ADHD and 19% of the youth with a history of mania were not on any medications. This raised doubts about the overall appropriateness of medication use in children within the child welfare system, with concerns about both overuse and underuse.

This body of research was the impetus for federal legislation requiring states to track and monitor psychotropic drug use among children in care. Provisions in the Fostering Connections to Success and Increasing Adoptions Act of 2008 mandated that state child welfare agencies develop plans for ongoing oversight of mental health services and psychotropic drug use. States were required to coordinate with Medicaid, and elicit input from specialists to develop a system to track prescription drug use in children in care.[122] The Child and Family Services Improvement and Innovation Act of 2011 amended this law by requiring states to develop protocols, not just for the monitoring of psychotropic medications, but for their appropriate uses as well.[123]

Three federal agencies, the Administration for Children and Families (ACF), Centers for Medicare and Medicaid Services (CMS), and the Substance Abuse and Mental Health Services Administration (SAMHSA) joined forces to help states achieve these mandates and develop plans for the effective management of psychotropic medication use among children in foster care. In 2012, ACF, CMS, and SAMHSA convened state child welfare, Medicaid, and mental health authorities to address the use of psychotropic medications in children involved with the child welfare system. All three agencies also have been providing ongoing support to states in these efforts via (1) posting online resources—webinars and Internet resources available through the ACF Child Welfare Gateway;[124] (2) distributing best practice guidelines for psychotropic use developed by the American Academy of Child and Adolescent Psychiatry; (3) working with States to enhance drug utilization review and promote the use of health technology, and in some cases, providing Medicaid incentive payments to providers who adopt, implement, or upgrade certified electronic health records technology; (4) disseminating exemplary practices from around the country; and (5) providing ongoing technical assistance to meet the federal mandates. In addition to assuring the appropriate use of psychotropic medications, states also are supposed to create a balanced array of services for children who are experiencing trauma-related behavioral health problems, with a strong focus on developing the infrastructure and local expertise to provide empirically validated psychosocial treatments.[125,126] (See References 124–126 for relevant resources.)

But what is the appropriate use of psychotropic medications in maltreated children? The database steering the existing guidelines is limited. As discussed in the treatise following Chapter 1, when compared with individuals who meet criteria for the diagnosis of major depression without a history of child abuse, individuals with a history of child abuse who meet criteria for depression are less likely to remit following standard evidence-based pharmacological (e.g., selective serotonin reuptake inhibitor medications like Prozac) interventions.[8] Individuals with a history of child maltreatment also appear to have a poorer treatment response across a range of diagnoses.[9] Although there have been numerous randomized controlled trials examining the efficacy of psychotherapeutic interventions in foster care children, there have only been three pharmacological treatment trials in children with PTSD.[127–129] These studies all examined different medications, and no definitive benefits of the adjunctive pharmacotherapy were demonstrated in any of the studies.[127–129]

The bottom line is the drugs are being used without a truly adequate research database to guide clinical practice. At the conclusion of the first paper, published in 1999, which examined psychotropic drug use in children in foster care, the authors cautioned that further research was needed to examine the appropriateness and level of benefit of medication treatment for children in foster care.[117] This conclusion continues to hold true more than a decade and a half later.

Would adherence to the current practice parameters have prevented Sylar's rehospitalization and subsequent placement in residential care? During the course of Sylar's time in care, more than one provider diagnosed Maria with bipolar disorder. The American Academy of Child and Adolescent Psychiatry (AACAP) Practice Parameters for the Treatment of Depression in Children and Adolescents published in 2007 recommends close monitoring for the development of manic symptoms when prescribing antidepressants to children with a family history of bipolar disorder, and costarting a mood stabilizer, such as lithium, to prevent the onset of manic episodes if risk for bipolar disorder is strongly suspected.[130]

Unfortunately these practice parameters did not exist when Sylar first initiated medication treatment for depression. Has the integration of AACAP practice parameters into child welfare appropriate psychotropic use guidelines made a difference for the kids in the system today? That is the hope. Systematic evaluation of the outcome of these policy changes, however, is still forthcoming.

Now back to our story, and an update on what has been going on with Samya.

11

No More Goody Two Shoes

(1,148 DAYS IN OUT-OF-HOME CARE)

Samya's new worker Jane (DCF-W10) is sitting at a table in the staff lounge with Monica (DCF-W7), updating her on what is happening with Samya. Sylar is still working with Barry (DCF-W9), but after working with her previous worker Lynn (DCF-W8) for six months, Samya was assigned another new worker—Jane (DCF-W10).

"How long was Samya at the treatment center after she got discharged from the hospital? I stopped working with her shortly after she got out of the hospital and first moved back there."

"Three months at the Safe Home, and just a bit over a year in the treatment center residential program."

"How'd she do there?"

"Generally pretty well. Some problems with oppositional behavior and aggression, usually when her mother's phone got disconnected, or a visit with her brother got canceled."

"Any additional hospitalizations?"

"She only had one brief hospitalization the whole time she was at the treatment center. It was while she was still in the Safe Home. She became acutely suicidal after a resident climbed in her bed while she was sleeping and started to unsnap his pants—but she was only in for a few days."

"Where is she now?"

"I just dropped her off yesterday at Howe Street group home. She seems to be adjusting pretty well. I didn't think she'd end up at a group home, but in the end, that's what she said she wanted. She was clear all along during our discharge planning that she did not want a foster home with a lot of kids. It looked like she was going to get to go back to her first foster placement with the Olsens, and she was excited about that, but the agency placed two other boys in the home, so that wasn't an option. Then I thought her mentor was going to get licensed as a foster care provider, but her mentor never finished the training."

"Did I hear someone say that Samya had surgery just a few weeks ago?

"Yeah. She had a breast neoplasm. It was benign."

"Wow. Who went with her for the surgery?"

"Her two favorite staff from the treatment center—Miss Pam and Lamont. She said Lamont walked her into the operating room and stayed with her until they started the anesthesia, and that he was by her side when she woke up. She said when it was time to leave the hospital, he pushed her in the wheelchair, lifted her up when she got to the car, and placed a pillow between her chest and the seatbelt when he strapped her in. She's going to miss those two; she told me they were like a mom and dad to her."

"When you see her next, tell her I say, 'hello.'"

"I will."

After Monica leaves the staff lounge, Jane thinks about her conversation with Samya after her last visit with Sylar. He greeted her with a dozen roses. She asked him, "Are these for my surgery?" He said, "What surgery?" He had bought them because he missed seeing her for her birthday. Both kids were mad that Sylar was not even told that Samya was having surgery. Jane thinks she will need to keep Barry in the loop about things that are going on with Samya.

The new group home where Samya is staying is a three-story white Victorian home. Samya's room is on the second floor above the staff office. She shares her room with two other girls. At the first treatment conference at the group home at the end of the summer, about two months after Samya moved into the home, the staff says Samya is having trouble adjusting.

"She's been verbally aggressive on a few occasions."

They also review an incident that happened the week prior with Shannon, the case aide who first drove Samya when she went to live with the Olsens, who used to drive her for visits with her mother, and who has been driving her for visits with Sylar since the two were separated after leaving the Olsens home a year and a half ago.

"Shannon said Samya was very disrespectful, cursing her out on the car ride back from the visit, and yelling at her for making her late for a phone call with her boyfriend. Shannon refuses to drive Samya any more."

After hearing this, Jane turns to Samya and asks, "Don't you think you need to apologize to Shannon?"

Samya replies, "No," with an attitude. "I think she was purposely driving slowly just so I'd miss my call. I don't care if she doesn't want to drive me any more."

After the meeting, Jane and Samya talk about Maria. Samya says she worries about her mom all the time.

The other girls at the group home start school the following week. There is a two-week delay in getting Samya enrolled due to administrative red tape. Samya has not been to public school since she lived with Tori.

Her first week at Fisher High School, Samya smokes her first joint with some kids after school. She says it did not affect her much. She smokes a second time while out on a date the following weekend. Walking down the street before going into the movies after getting high, Samya falls three times. The last time she has trouble getting up.

The guy she is with says jokingly, "I am going to leave you here if you don't get up."

When she gets up, he helps her get rocks out of her hair and then they both go into the movies. They leave early enough to stop at the Rite Aid before she is picked up by the staff at the group home. Samya sprays herself with perfume so the staff at her home will not be able to smell the weed. When she gets in the car, the staff member comments, "Whew, you really sprayed yourself good! You must like the way that stuff smells."

Over the next few weeks, Samya's problems with her moods and behavior escalate. One night she is in her room agitated. She puts a CD and her headsets on, sits on her bed, and tries to chill. Music has always helped calm her down. A staff member comes in and tells her to put the CD player away and clean her room. She says, "No," turns her back to the staff and thinks, *Miss Pam and Lamont know when I need my music and my space. Leave me the fuck alone.*

The staff grabs her headphones and takes the CD player from the bed, saying, "You just lost the privilege to use your CD player for a week."

Samya turns around, jumps up, and grabs the small wooden chair by the side of her bed. Without thinking she throws the chair against the wall. It breaks into several pieces and leaves a huge dent in the wall.

Two other staff come running into the room. One helps the first staff restrain Samya, and the other staff goes downstairs to call the police. A few minutes later a gruff fifty-something police officer arrives, handcuffs Samya, and escorts her down the stairs while the other girls in the house gawk.

When Samya gets to the police station she is thrown into a small holding cell. She sits on the cot shaking, having trouble believing she is where she is.

The police officer calls the DCF hotline and arranges for an on-call worker to pick her up and bring her back to the group home. Three hours pass before the worker arrives. Samya does not talk to the on-call worker on her way back to the group home, and she does not talk to the night staff when she gets back to the house. In a haze, she walks up the stairs to her room and climbs in bed with her clothes still on.

Over the next few weeks, problems spill over to school. Samya is suspended twice and an emergency Planning and Placement Team (PPT) meeting is scheduled at the school.

Sitting around the table for the PPT meeting are Mrs. M., the Director of Special Education at Fisher High, Mrs. T., the Director of New Start, the self-contained special education program housed at Fisher High School, Mr.

P., the surrogate parent appointed by the Department of Education, Jane, and Samya. The bell rings just after the last person arrives for the meeting, and the hallway swells with hordes of students. The noise filters in through the conference room door, so Mrs. M. waits for the ruckus to die down before starting the meeting. Samya rests her head on the table while they wait. Her black hood is pulled up so her face is barely visible. Practically all that shows are the multiple piercings on her earlobe, nose, and eyebrow.

At the start of the meeting, Mrs. M. asks everyone to state his or her name for the record. When it is Samya's turn to speak, she lifts her head and says, "I'm nobody."

After hearing this, Jane leans over and gives Samya's arm a gentle rub. She whispers something in her ear, and a slight smile comes across Samya's face.

As the updates are given describing Samya's decline since the start of the new school year—the suspensions for fighting with peers and cursing at teachers, and the dime bag of marijuana she was caught with at school—Samya lets her mind drift. She thinks about her mother. She wishes her mother were at the meeting. The last time she tried to call from therapy, her mother's phone was disconnected.

When Mrs. M. asks Samya what she thinks she needs to succeed, Samya sits up. She pushes her hood down, and unfolds a two-page letter she prepared for the meeting. She looks younger and more innocent with her flat-ironed hair, bronzed skin, and big cat-shaped eyes exposed.

Samya talks about knowing she got in with the wrong crowd when she came to Fisher High School. After being at the residential treatment center practically on lock down, she was not used to the freedom. She talks about the small classrooms she had when she was in the residential treatment program, and says she thinks she needs something more like that. She also talks about being scared by her drug use; scared she will end up an addict like her mother.

Everyone agrees that the New Start self-contained program with small classes and daily counseling is a better fit for her. Samya is relieved to get a second chance; she had feared she would be expelled and be out of school for the year. On the way out of the conference room, she asks Jane if they can go for ice cream to celebrate.

A few weeks later, Jane and a staff member from the group home accompany Samya to her pretrial hearing for the chair-throwing incident. They meet with the public defender in a small musty office outside the courtroom. He lets them know the prosecutor offered 20 hours of community service to be completed by Christmas. All agree and sign the necessary paperwork.

Jane, the staff, and Samya then go out for something to eat.

"Have you talked with my mom lately?"

"Barry and I met with her a few weeks ago in her new apartment back in New York, but neither of us has heard from her since. I don't think she has a phone yet."

Samya begins to cry. "There's a part of me that's used to this shit from her, but it still hurts every time. Who doesn't have a phone?" She then looks down and says, "She's never gonna change."

Three weeks after this meeting, Jane gets a request to pick Samya up from school because she is sick and there is no group home staff available to pick her up. When she walks into the nurse's office she sees Samya lying down on the cot in the back room. She introduces herself and shows her ID to the school nurse.

"Samya's been sick a lot lately, complaining of bad headaches and stomach aches. Her teachers also have complained that she's been falling asleep in class."

"Thanks for taking such good care of her."

Samya pops her head up as Jane walks into the back room.

"Ready to go?"

Samya sits up and puts her shoes on. She and Jane walk out of school together. On the car ride home Jane gives Samya a new phone number for Maria, and lets Samya know she has a visit scheduled with her brother for the following day.

"I haven't seen my brother in four months since the summer."

"Yeah, it has been too long. There's a new case aide, Barbara. She'll be driving you."

Barbara picks Samya up at school at the end of the following day, and Samya is quiet for most of the hour-long ride to Sylar's residential treatment center in New York. When Barbara pulls up to the administrative building of the residential treatment center, Sylar is waiting on the front steps. Samya pops out of the car and gives Sylar a heartfelt hug. The three then go into the administrative building, sign in, and walk to Sylar's therapist's office.

Sylar's therapist, Paul, has worked at the residential treatment center for almost 20 years. He has a neatly trimmed beard speckled with gray and warm blue eyes that immediately put one at ease. When they reach his office, he lets Barbara and Samya know they are going to call Maria.

"I knew Samya had a scheduled telephone call with her mother tomorrow at her therapist's office. I didn't know there were any plans to call her today."

"It's been a while since she's had a working number, so Sylar was eager to call her and thought it would be good to call while Samya is here. We can call using the speaker phone, and I'll be here throughout to supervise the call."

As both children greet their mother, the years of hurt and disappointment are absent from their voices and their expressions.

Maria asks, "Samya, how are you?"

"Good. I am really good."

"I heard you were arrested. I am so proud of you!"

Paul exclaims, "Being arrested is not a good thing."

"I know. It's just that Samya was always such a goody two shoes."

"Why don't you all talk about something else?"

Maria starts reminiscing about when they were all living together back in New York. As she talks, Sylar passes a piece of paper to Samya with their brother Gregory's name on it. Samya gets a stunned look on her face and answers haphazardly to Maria's banter. She then interrupts her mother.

"Did you know Sylar is trying to find Gregory?"

"Yeah, he told me."

Paul interjects, "I told him it was going to be a long uphill battle, but no one listens to me."

The call lasts about 10 minutes, and then Barbara takes the kids to Wendy's for the remainder of their one-hour visit.

The next treatment conference at the group home is two weeks after Samya's visit with Sylar. Jane notes that Samya looks happier than she has seen her in a good long time.

"There's been a remarkable turnaround in Samya's behavior over the past 10 days."

"I've been sleeping better, and I think it definitely helped to talk with my ma."

Samya lets Jane know that for two weeks in a row she got a certificate at school for being the most respectful in class. She also just started working at Shaw's supermarket. They talk about the telephone call with Maria. Samya says she knew about her brother Gregory, but that it bothered her a bit to talk about him. She also says she knows that it was inappropriate for her mother to call her a "goody two shoes," but she also thought it somewhat funny. They then talk about Christmas. Samya had a quiet Christmas at the house with the girls. She takes Jane up to her room to show her the things she got for Christmas, and while they are up in her room, Jane surprises Samya with a gift certificate and a stuffed animal.

Over the next few months, things are fairly stable. Samya is having monthly visits from Jane, and monthly telephone calls with her mother from her therapist's office. Her grades are good and she is making high honors. She goes two months without seeing Sylar, but her moods and behavior are stable until April.

In April, another breast neoplasm is found and Samya is scheduled for surgery again. Her mother is also a no-show for an in-person session that was scheduled with her therapist. Jane gets to the therapist's office shortly after Samya learned her mother would not be coming. When she first arrives, Samya is sitting on the floor, curled in a ball, tears streaming down her face.

Samya sits up and says, "I am giving up. I don't want any more telephone contact with my mother and I don't want to see her again. It is useless."

At the next treatment conference at the group home, staff members report, "Samya's behavior has gone downhill over the past two weeks. She's at the lowest level of privileges at the group home, and she tested positive for marijuana again last week."

School suspensions re-start within a few weeks, and Samya is angry and threatening to sign herself out of DCF during most of her visits with Jane throughout the summer. Samya only sees Sylar once over the next four months, because she repeatedly loses visiting privileges due to her behavior.

Two weeks into the new school year, Samya and two other girls get up after the 9:30 bed check. They go to the bathroom on the side of the house opposite the staff office. They have multiple bed sheets in hand, which they tie together. They then tie one end of the sheets to the pole in the bathroom and quietly open the window. Pricilla is the first to shimmy down to the ground from the second-floor window. The other girl goes next, Samya last. They then walk down the street to the house of a guy named Mike— someone Pricilla knows. Mike hands out beers to everyone when they get inside, and everyone stays up late playing board games, listening to music, and drinking. Midday the following day, a friend of Pricilla's arrives to take her to Meriden. He is concerned when he sees the extra two girls at the house.

"I am not taking anyone else with us. They are all minors."

"I'm sorry you guys," says Pricilla.

"No worries, you go. We'll go back to the house in a bit."

That was Samya's first AWOL (Absence without Official Leave). There are two others over the next month and a half—one for five days, another for two days. Each time she returns she tests positive for marijuana. When she comes back the third time she is discharged from the group home, with plans for DCF to transfer her to an alternate group home program that specializes in substance abuse treatment in another part of the state. She lived at this group home for one year and three months; the new group home will be Samya's tenth placement since first entering care just over four years ago.

Congregate Care

Before discussing congregate care, the topic of this treatise, I want to comment briefly on the two breast tumors Samya developed. As noted at the end of Chapter 9, individuals with a history of abuse and other adverse early experiences are not just at increased risk for psychiatric and substance use disorders, but also at increased risk for cancer and a whole host of other health problems.[111,131] It is unusual that Samya developed these breast neoplasms at such a young age, but her development of them is consistent with the maltreatment-related epigenetic changes in genes linked to the development of breast tumors we observed in our research.[107] More work is needed to understand the mechanisms by which early adversity confers risk for various health problems, but our preliminary work suggests epigenetic mechanisms may be key.

Back to the topic of congregate care—in this brief treatise, the term congregate care is used to denote any group care living arrangement: both large- and small-scale institutions and group home settings. According to the most recently compiled federal statistics, approximately 58,000 children within the child welfare system are living in congregate care settings, an estimated 34,000 in institutions, and 24,000 in group homes.[132] This represents 15% of the foster care population in the United States,[132] with the proportion of foster children living in congregate care settings varying markedly across the nation, from a low of about 5% in Oregon and Washington State, to about 20% in Connecticut, and a high of about 30% in Wyoming and Colorado.

As we have seen in this book, the line between family care and group care can become somewhat blurred. Marla's home was technically a family foster-care placement, but it was certainly operated like a group home. Although having homes that can accommodate numerous children is helpful from an administrative perspective, the more unrelated children in a home, the less stable the placements.[67] This treatise focuses on officially designated congregate care placements, but many of the concerns raised are relevant to foster homes like Marla's, which house a large number of unrelated children.

At the time Sylar and Samya were in the system, rates of congregate care in Connecticut were about 20% higher than they are today, and approximately 500 youth were living in out-of-state residential treatment centers. There were a lot of youth like Sylar, isolated and languishing in high-end care settings. The number of children from Connecticut living in out-of-state residential placements dropped to 364 by 2011, and with a new administration in state government, and a commitment to "bring our kids home," in four years the number was down to 15. This is a remarkable achievement. Over the past four years in Connecticut, there have been systematic efforts to "right-size the system"—decrease the total number of children in care, and for those children who are removed from their parents' custody, increase the proportion of foster care and kinship care placements, and decrease use of congregate care settings.

Why are children placed in congregate care settings? When Sylar and Samya entered the system, at the time of their initial removal Connecticut was placing the majority of children in one of the Safe Homes group care facilities. The initial goal of the Safe Home program was to consolidate resources to enhance assessment and treatment planning to improve outcomes for children and families. Our research showed, however, that with placements at the Safe Home program lasting an average 45–60 days, the state was spending about an extra $10,000 per child without a lot of bang for its buck.[31] Consequently, Safe Home group programs are no longer being used routinely in Connecticut at time of initial placement.

At the time Sylar and Samya entered care, approximately one in five birth to five-year-old children in Connecticut initially were being placed in one of the Safe Home group care programs, even though the negative consequences of congregate care on young children were first documented more than five decades earlier.[133] In recent years, advocacy efforts have eliminated almost entirely the use of group care for very young children in Connecticut.

Currently congregate care settings most frequently are being used to accommodate children who have had one or more "failed" foster placements. As we have seen in this book, placement "failures" can be due to poor communication, but more often than not relate to children having significant, and frequently unmet, mental health care needs.

The United Nations Convention on the Rights of the Child, approved in 1989, asserts that the family is the fundamental group of society and the natural environment for the growth and well-being of children. It contends that families should be afforded the necessary protection and assistance so that they can fully assume their responsibilities, and if children are temporarily or permanently deprived of their families, or cannot be allowed to remain with their families for safety reasons, children are entitled to special protection and assistance by the State, which includes assurance of alternative care.[134] It is noteworthy, that as of this writing, the United States was one of only two nations worldwide, the other being South Sudan, to have not ratified the United Nations Convention of the Rights of the Child.

In 2009, in celebrating the 20th anniversary of the Convention of the Rights of the Child, the United Nations adopted a resolution delineating guidelines for alternative care for children deprived of parental care.[135] The resolution states that alternative care for young children, especially those under the age of three years, should be provided in family-based settings. In a recent policy paper, I and several colleagues took a stronger position, contending that institutional care is nonoptimal for children of all ages, including teenagers, and that even smaller group care settings can be detrimental to the growth and well-being of youth.[136]

In our policy paper we distinguish between group care used for a limited time as a respite or a time-limited therapeutic intervention with specific goals, and the use of group care as a place to live. One key distinction is that children in group treatment programs or psychiatric facilities usually retain an ongoing relationship with their parents or other adults who serve as guardians, with these adults ideally actively involved in the treatment. Youth living in group care, in contrast, rarely retain that kind of contact and usually have to rely on rotating staff to provide guidance and support.[136]

As noted several times throughout this book, attachment to a caring and stable adult caregiver is one of the most important factors to promote resiliency in maltreated children. Shift care, whether the shifts last hours or days, interferes with accessibility and attachment to caring adults. In addition, rules that protect against liability by prohibiting activities that would encourage a relationship between staff and youth are a further barrier,[136] although as we will see in Sylar's case, there are some group care personnel who break the mold and go above and beyond expectations long after discharge from the facility to provide ongoing support as needed.

Group care is often justified based on the therapeutic needs of the child, and implemented for children with substance abuse problems, sexual acting out behavior, or delinquency, but in the majority of cases, these problems can be safely and effectively treated in the community.[80,137,138] Although there are indications in which psychiatric hospitalization or locked care facilities may be briefly necessary for safety, most serious problems can be treated effectively with clinic or home-based interventions.[136]

Some literature even suggests that congregate care may lead to deviant outcomes. Ryan and colleagues conducted a large-scale study comparing youth in group care settings to an extremely well-matched sample of youth living in foster care.[139] The samples were matched on race, sex, abuse and placement history, presence of behavior problems, and history of running away. After controlling for all these factors, youth placed in group care settings were 2.4 times more likely to be arrested, suggesting that group care per se, may increase the likelihood of delinquency and criminal activity. It has been hypothesized that contagion effects and an absence of positive role models may contribute to this phenomenon. Do you think Samya would have shimmied down to the ground from a second floor window in the middle of the night and gone AWOL if she were still living with the Olsens?

As discussed at the end of Chapter 8, there also are data to suggest that children in congregate care are at higher risk of abuse than children in foster care placements. The study comparing the prevalence of maltreatment in foster and residential care to the prevalence in the general population found that sexual abuse, including incidents of peer and adult initiated contact, was higher in residential care than in either foster care or the general population.[89] There was no difference in the incidence of sexual abuse between foster care and the general population. The rate of self-reported physical abuse in residential care was almost double that of foster care, and it was triple the rate reported in the general population of same-age adolescents surveyed.[88] A large majority of group care workers in residential settings also suffer from violence due to behavior management issues,[140] adding to the toxicity of congregate care settings.

The Annie E. Casey Foundation has been working with various jurisdictions to help in "rightsizing congregate care." Their action plan has four primary goals: (1) Reduce congregate beds; (2) Increase community foster homes; (3) Increase community-based services; and (4) Increase use of kinship placements for children.[141] Sylar recently asked me why DCF never explored the option of having him and Samya live with one of their relatives; in reality, they have more than nine aunts and three uncles. It is a travesty that these family resources were never explored, given that some of his relatives would have made optimal caregivers. (See Reference 136 for an elaboration on these issues and Reference 141 for strategies for rightsizing congregate care.)

As summarized in our position paper,

> Every child has a basic right and need to grow up in a safe home with a stable continuous relationship with at least one adult who is a trusted, committed parent figure. Group settings should not be used as living arrangements, because of their inherently detrimental effects on the healthy development of children, regardless of age. Group care should be used for children only when it is the least detrimental alternative. That standard is met only when there is no less restrictive setting available to meet a child's need for therapeutic mental health services. Even in that instance, group care should end when it ceases to be the least detrimental alternative for that child.[136]

For the last two-plus years, Samya and Sylar were committed to the custody of the State; they were denied this fundamental basic right.

12

Turning Eighteen

(1,614 DAYS IN OUT-OF-HOME CARE)

Sylar lives at the residential treatment center in New York for two years and ten months. In the first year he is there, his DCF worker, Barry, visits six times, and Samya visits ten times. In the second year he is there, Barry visits eight times, and Samya visits six times. In the last ten months he is at the center, Barry visits eight times and Samya visits twice. There are lots of times throughout his stay at the residential treatment center that Sylar feels alone and lost.

In his first six months in the program, every time he meets with Barry he says he is going to sign himself out of DCF care when he turns sixteen. By one year, residential staff describe him as a "leader in the program." He has no significant behavior problems throughout his stay at the center. He never gets out of control; he never requires restraint.

This is not true of the other kids at the residential treatment center. Sylar sees a lot of kids get out of control and require restraints. It happens almost every day, some days it happens multiple times. He gets somewhat numb to it. There are a lot of bad incidents while he is at the center, but the one that occurs about seven months before he leaves is the worst.

The day begins like any typical fall school day. Sylar stares out the classroom window, his chin resting in the palm of his hand. His science teacher measures some liquid, describing step by step the tedious lab procedure they are about to begin. He half listens to the instructions.

Sylar hears Bill mumbling in the seat to the right of him, but tries to ignore him. Bill is agitated. Bill gets up and starts pacing. Mr. Phelps asks him to leave the classroom and go back to his unit if he cannot stay in his seat.

Bill replies, "You gonna make me? What the fuck you gonna do?"

Bill then approaches Mr. Phelps's desk, and in a split second he has the metal stool by the side of Mr. Phelps's desk up over his head.

Smash. The glass flask on Mr. Phelps's desk flies across the room.

Smash again. The stool comes down hard on Mr. Phelps's head and blood gushes everywhere. Mr. Phelps falls to the ground.

Sylar springs from his chair and grabs the stool as Bill winds up for another shot. He throws the stool to the far side of the class, and pushes Bill out of the room, locking the door behind him.

After he closes the door, Sylar can hear the shouts and racing feet of multiple staff from down the hall. Bill curses, and there is a loud thud as the staff take him down to the ground.

There are only five other kids in the class. Sylar suggests that one of the other kids go out the back door of the classroom to get the nurse. Sylar gets some paper towels and begins applying pressure to the gash on Mr. Phelps's head.

Mr. Phelps has a concussion and requires 40 stitches. He is OK, but he never comes back to work at the residential treatment center after that day.

Two weeks after the incident in the classroom, the local police department holds a ceremony in Sylar's honor. It is a crisp autumn day, late in the afternoon. The orange and yellow leaves reflect brightly in the lake at the perimeter of campus. A tent is set up on the main field at the residential treatment center and everyone is there for the event, including all the staff, students, and four members of the police department. Sylar is presented with a plaque for his bravery. Paul, Sylar's therapist, beams in the corner throughout the ceremony.

Paul is critical to getting Sylar through his nearly three years at the residential treatment center. For the entire time that Sylar is at the center, he meets twice weekly with Paul, usually once in his office, and once out in the community. It took over a year for Sylar to start trusting Paul, but Paul was patient. They develop a ritual of going for "Spicy Chicken Therapy." There are days Paul arrives on the unit to pick up Sylar and Paul can tell by Sylar's demeanor that he needs more than just a trip to his office on the other side of campus. He asks, "What do you say, is it a Spicy Chicken Therapy day?" That elicits a smile from Sylar, and they then trek off to Paul's car for a trip to Wendy's. Sylar orders a #6, Spicy Chicken, just mayo, and a coke, and Paul usually gets a chocolate frosty.

A few months after the police ceremony, Paul and Sylar start planning for Sylar's discharge. When Paul gets to the unit to pick Sylar up for therapy, he finds him sitting on the couch in the common room, playing video games with another boy on the unit. Sylar grabs his coat and they begin walking across the chilly campus to Paul's office. It is a cold February day and there is an inch or so of snow on the ground.

As they walk across campus Paul says, "I got a call from Barry today. Everything is now set for you to stay at the center through the end of the school year, a few months after you turn 18."

"Did he say anything about what the plan is after that?"

"He said he's hoping to schedule a time for you and I to go see a program for young adults in Norwich, Connecticut."

"No offense, but I'm kinda sick of programs."

"It sounds like it has a lot of good resources. You'd have your own apartment, but there'd be staff to help you out with things. You could finish high school, stay in treatment, and be around other kids your age."

"I may just sign myself out of the system and go and live with my mother."

"You don't have to make any decisions now. Hey, I also spoke to your mom earlier today. She's expecting our call this afternoon."

"OK."

When they get to Paul's office, Sylar plops down on the couch and looks out the window. Paul puts the phone on the table between them and pulls out the file with Maria's phone number.

The phone rings four times before Maria answers. There's a crash on the other end of the line as she picks up.

"Shit.... Uh, hello?"

"You clumsy woman, what did you just knock over?"

"The table with the phone." Maria's speech is somewhat slurred and she is talking too loudly. Sylar looks across at Paul.

"Hi Maria, this is Paul and Sylar. Is it still a good time to talk?"

"Yeah, I was expectin' your call."

"Are you high Ma?"

"No, just flustered cuz I ran 'cross the room and knocked over da table."

Sylar thinks, *Bullshit*. "Listen, Paul and I gotta go. Something came up. We'll talk another time."

"Alright, my monkey boy. Maybe next week."

Sylar gets up and starts pacing in the office. He has tears in his eyes.

"Want to go for a walk?"

Sylar nods, unable to speak.

They walk in silence down the pathway toward the frozen lake.

"She's never gonna change."

"Probably not." Paul thinks about the many times he has ridden this roller coaster with Sylar.

"I'm cutting her off."

"You have to focus on you and your plans. Maybe we can get up to Connecticut next week and check out that program." Paul cannot count the number of times over the years that Sylar has flip-flopped between threatening to sign himself out of DCF and go live with his mother, and saying he is never going to talk with her again.

When Paul goes to Sylar's unit the next week to pick him up, he finds Sylar sitting in the corner of the common room by himself. Two other boys are sitting on the couch playing video games.

"How are you doing?"

Sylar looks up in a daze. He had lost track of the time.

"You look tired."

"I didn't sleep much last night. I had a dream about my mother's ex- who messed with me."

"That's in the past. We have to focus on your future."

Sylar does not reply. He grabs his coat from the chair behind him and starts walking toward the door.

"I got some brochures for the program."

Sylar does not comment.

"We're scheduled to go visit next Tuesday."

Sylar acknowledges what Paul says with a nod.

"You in the mood for Spicy Chicken Therapy?"

Sylar smiles. "That would be great."

They walk to Paul's car and drive off to Wendy's.

A few days later, the trip to the program in Norwich is positive overall. On the car ride back to the center Sylar reads the program brochure.

Young Adult Services is an assertive community treatment program designed to provide young people (18–25 years of age) who are "aging out" of the Department of Children and Families support with their integration into the community. An interdisciplinary clinical team provides services that help individuals maximize their potential, abide by society's laws and norms, and respect the rights and integrity of others in the community.

Sylar muses, *What do they think I am? Some kind of derelict who's going to break the law and disrespect others?* He reads on.

Most individuals are provided with assistance in establishing a living situation, clinical services, and assistance with education and/or vocational planning. In addition, many young people receive assistance in developing independent living skills and are helped to develop appropriate recreational pursuits.

Sylar's 18th birthday is coming up. He already has been in the system almost five years. He thinks to himself, *Am I going to stay in the system another seven years until I am 25?*

Over the next few months plans for discharge to the Young Adult Program move forward; Sylar can go live there after the school year ends. He retains his doubts but keeps them to himself.

One afternoon in late April while Laura, the housemother, is busy with some other kids upstairs, Sylar goes into her office and calls his mother.

"Hey."

"Hey. How are you? It was your birthday last week. Eighteen years old!"

"Yeah." Sylar thinks, *Yup, it was another birthday in care.*

"Stanley has a car. Want me to drive up and pick you up? It is time for you to come home."

"I don't know. If I can, I'll call you tomorrow. I gotta go."

Sylar hangs up the phone and goes to his bedroom.

The next afternoon Paul is surprised to find Sylar and Maria outside his office door.

"I'm taking my boy home."

"What about finishing the school year?"

"I can finish school from my mom's house."

"What about the program? What brought about this change?"

"I don't know. It is just time for me to leave."

"My boy is finally coming home." Maria does not share any of Sylar's hesitations.

With little further discussion, some papers are signed, and Paul walks Sylar out to Maria's car. He escorts them to the unit and stays while Sylar packs his things, hoping Sylar will have a change of heart. When the car is fully loaded, Sylar walks over to Paul and gives him a hug.

"Thanks for all you did for me. I will keep in touch."

"Do, definitely do. ... If you change your mind, the Young Adult Program will still be an option for you."

Paul stands in the road as Sylar and Maria drive off. Befuddled, he stands looking at the roadway out of the center long after they are gone. He did not see this ending coming.

Emancipation

Approximately 25,000 children are emancipated, or "age-out" of the foster care system each year.[142] Of these youth, approximately 25% were age 12 years or younger when they entered care,[60] and approximately one-third experienced eight or more placements before aging out.[62] Many, like Sylar, resume relationships with their birth families. They have no one else.

The outcomes for children who age out of the foster care system are rather abysmal.[143,144] More than one in five will become homeless at some point, with some studies estimating rates more than twice that high;[145] only 58% will graduate high school by age 19, compared with 87% of all 19-year-olds; 71% of young women who age out of the system will be pregnant by age 21; only half of youth will be employed at the age of 24; fewer than 3% will earn a college degree by age 25, compared with 28% of all 25-year-olds; and one in four will be involved with the justice system within two years of leaving the foster care system.[146]

Over the past several decades, a series of legislative Acts have been passed to help states improve the outcomes of youth aging out of the system.[147] In 1985, the Independent Living Initiative (Public Law 99-272) was passed to provide funds to states under Title IV-E of the Social Security Act to help youth develop skills needed for independent living. Funding was reauthorized in 1993 (Public Law 103-66).[147] Basic services outlined in the law include outreach programs, training in daily living skills, education and employment assistance, counseling, and case management. Federal funds could not, however, be used for room and board, so the Foster Care Independence Act of 1999 (Public Law 106-169) was passed to create the Chafee Foster Care Independence Program, giving states more funding and greater flexibility in providing support for youths making the transition to independent living. The Foster Care Independence Act doubled federal independent living services funding to $140 million per year, and allowed states to use up to 30% of these funds for room and board.[147] In 2002, the Educational and Training Vouchers Program for Youths Aging out of Foster Care was added to the Chafee Foster Care Independence Program.[148] The Vouchers Program provides resources specifically to meet the education and training needs of youth aging out of foster care. In addition, the Fostering Connections to Success and Increasing Adoptions Act of 2008 allowed states to extend foster care and receive federal IV-E reimbursement (under Title IV-E of the Social Security Act) on behalf of youth up to age 21. As of 2015, 23 states have taken advantage of these resources and extended the age for foster care eligibility,[144] with all states currently providing some support services to young people 18 and older through the federal Chafee Foster Care Independence Program. The level of services, however, varies dramatically among states.

Optimal intervention programs for youth aging out of the system aim to[143] (1) promote stable, permanent connections to caring adults; (2) assist youth with the management of their physical and mental health needs; (3) support economic success through education and employment programs; (4) provide life skills training to help youth navigate the adult world; (5) improve access to stable and safe housing; and (6) facilitate cross-system collaborations between the child welfare system and other youth-serving systems, such as workforce development, postsecondary education, mental health, and the justice system. Many states also have created mechanisms for youth to provide input on state policies and programs affecting children aging out of the system.

In May 2013, the Jim Casey Youth Opportunities Initiative launched a national campaign focusing on youth aging out of the system.[144] A central tenet of the Jim Casey initiative is young people in foster care should not be on their own when they turn 18, or even when they turn 21. The Jim Casey initiative, *Success Beyond 18*, leverages insights from research and practice, and highlights federal funding opportunities for states to use to create better opportunities for youth aging out of the system to succeed in school, work, and family life.

The Jim Casey Foundation conducted a cost analysis to generate a business case for investing in youth aging out of the foster care system.[146] They investigated the financial implications of improving the outcomes of youth on a number of important, and potentially expensive, poor indicators common among children who exit the foster care system. Focusing just on high school graduation rates, teen pregnancy, unemployment, and criminal justice involvement, the Foundation estimated that the outcome differences between youth transitioning from foster care and youth in the general population costs nearly $8 billion for each annual cohort of youth leaving care. They argue effectively that the cost of inaction is exorbitant. (See References 143, 144, and 146 for detailed descriptions of various policies and programs being implemented to improve the outcomes of youth aging out of the system.)

13

Epilogue

Within six months of Sylar returning home, before the close of 2006, Samya signs herself out of the system and goes to live with Maria. It is not long before Samya is deeply disappointed.

Early one morning Samya sits on the couch in the living room facing the apartment door. She has been up all night. The sun has long since risen and Samya feels like a grenade about to explode. Sylar is still asleep in the adjacent room.

At last the front door opens. Maria quietly enters the apartment, smelling of smoke, a contrite expression on her face. Samya sends the mug she is holding in her hand crashing against the wall behind Maria.

"What the fuck is wrong with you?" Maria squeals.

"What the fuck is wrong with me?"

Samya approaches her mom, tears streaming down her face. She resists the urge to strike Maria and begins pacing back and forth.

"You try to sneak your sorry ass in here high as a kite and think Sylar and I don't know what shit you been up to."

Samya turns away from her mother and freezes. Images of life with her mom when she was a kid flood through her mind. The sex for drugs, smoke-filled rooms, and her mother hooking up with one violent partner after another.

Samya shakes her head as if to loosen the grip of the past and bring herself back to the present. "I have had it. I am not putting up with this crap anymore. You quit that shit or I swear to God, you will never see me again."

Although Maria has heard this ultimatum before, there is a determination in Samya's voice that makes Maria believe Samya really means it this time. This really scares Maria. She worries that she might lose Samya for good, and then she wonders if she has already lost her.

Samya walks toward the front door. "Do you know how many times I defended you? They were right. You don't care about anything but your drugs." She pauses, then adds, "I'm done." Her hurt is deafening.

Samya opens the door and begins to walk out. Maria reaches for her arm, but Samya breaks free in one quick jerk.

She looks hard at her mother and reiterates in a cold and calculated tone, "I said I am done."

Samya slams the door as she leaves. Maria crumbles to the floor. After a few minutes Maria notices Sylar standing at the entrance to the living room looking down at her.

This fight is a wake up call to Maria. She quits crack cocaine cold turkey. No program, no sponsor. As Maria later told me when describing her resolve to quit, "I just couldn't take looking at their disappointed eyes any longer."

The changes for the positive are solidified by a chance encounter with Teddy, Maria's old close friend from high school who helped give her the strength she needed to leave her grandparents' house as a teen. Teddy and Maria were friends for over 20 years, but in the years the children were in care, they lost touch. At the time Teddy runs into Maria, he, too, is using and trying to turn his life around. He is working with his pastor to maintain sobriety, and one day he prays to see Maria again. Although they had never been romantically involved, Teddy says he always loved Maria. Once again, if this were fiction, a reader would tell me that what happens is too contrived—but literally the day after he prays to run into Maria, Teddy bumps into her at the bus station.

2010

When I began working on this project in 2010, it was four years after that chance encounter. Teddy and Maria were still together, both still sober, and Maria was enjoying her first healthy relationship. At that point in time everyone was in New York. Sylar was in a monogamous relationship with a girl he met at the library, living in an apartment about 15 minutes from Maria and Teddy. Samya was also in a committed relationship, and living with her boyfriend and one-year-old son with Maria and Teddy. Maria doted on her grandson, whom she affectionately called "Dado," and spoiled him in ways she missed out on with her own kids. At an interview with Maria at that time she said to me:

> I still have nightmares that I'm doing drugs. I dream that Teddy left me for someone else because I went back to drugs, and my kids won't bother with me because I am a crack head again. I wake up pissed off, upset that I let my family down again. I then realize, "Shit, it's just a dream." I reach across the bed, rub Teddy's leg, and say to myself, "He's here. Dado and Samya are across the hall, and Sylar is at home across town." I then roll over and I go back to sleep.

2015

Sometime within this past year, Maria relapsed. She sold Teddy's flat screen TV, Dado's PlayStation, and stole cash from Sylar and Samya. After months of her lying about her drug use, Teddy finally moved out.

Samya is twenty-six now and has three boys, all with the same father. Unfortunately, over the course of their relationship he has become increasingly violent. Samya is working part-time at a minimum wage job. For a while she was in a dual diagnosis program addressing her problems with alcohol, depression, and PTSD, but now she is just struggling to get by. She has hopes of leaving her partner someday, but she is not ready yet.

Sylar attained his GED and still sees Paul a few times a year. Paul has been at the other end of the phone line many a time when Sylar needed a rational, supportive sounding board. Sylar is also working part time at a minimum wage job, and is applying for Social Security benefits, as he has been unable to maintain a full-time job over the years. He had no health insurance when he left the system, and has only recently restarted on medication and in mental health treatment. This spring Sylar plans to get married. He is in a different relationship than he was back in 2010, but it is a strong positive relationship. He and his fiancé are currently living with Maria, but they are hoping to get their own place soon. Sylar wants desperately to get away from his mother.

An Untold Unconfirmed Story

When I did my last interview for this book with Sylar at the beginning of 2015, I asked him if he felt comfortable discussing his history of sexual abuse, given that it was described rather vaguely in the records. He shared more about the ex-boyfriend who messed with him and Samya when they were four and five, and he also said his mom prostituted him and Samya when they were preteens. He said he and Samya told some schoolteachers about this, and they were taken into custody briefly before their mom moved them to Connecticut. This information is nowhere in the Connecticut records, and nowhere in the records I had from New York. When I met with Mrs. Olsen, however, she said the kids told her their mom had sold them; I thought she was mistaken.

Sylar asked me to try to get his New York records. I submitted the request.

When I followed up by telephone with the person who sent me the release form, she said she needed to check with her supervisor. She said she would likely be able to share information about the kids' placement history, but stated that they do not usually share specific information about abuse or neglect. When I sent an e-mail a few days later to this person and copied the other person in her office in charge of records, she e-mailed her colleague, "We are all set with this N. I have the file and release and someone will be reaching out to her (Kaufman) shortly."

I then received the following e-mail message from the Chief Legal Counsel:

> Dr. Kaufman,
>
> I am in receipt of your request for information and accompanying release. I am also aware that you previously obtained records for the sibling, [Gregory] from this department. There are no other records pertaining to the child, [Sylar].
>
> Specifically, 1) there is no information regarding "prostituting" of children by mother; and 2) there are no other records regarding foster home, group home or other placements.

Both Sylar and Samya remember a brief group home placement shortly before moving to Connecticut. Samya says she does not remember why they were removed, and states most of the memories from her childhood are muddled.

If there were no records, why didn't the first person I dealt with just tell me that? Are there records they are choosing not to release? Did Maria prostitute the children? If so, why were they returned to her after a brief stay in care?

I have to confess it has been hard to interact with Maria since learning about this potential piece of history. I thought about asking her about it, but she is in addict mind now, and there are few truths that pass her lips. I asked Paul, and he said he does not know exactly what happened to Sylar; he just knows there was physical and sexual abuse. In his treatment, he did not go into the details of Sylar's past traumatic experiences, but instead tried to encourage Sylar to leave the past in the past and focus on the present and the future.

Ninety-nine percent of me finds Sylar's report completely plausible, especially given Mrs. Olsen's recollection of the children telling her about this, and the odd correspondences about the existence or nonexistence of relevant records. One percent of me holds on to the hope that it is not true.

An Apology to the Reader

I apologize for not giving you a warning before the 2015 update. I should have given you the option to skip that update in the preceding section and move directly to the next chapter. I decided, however, not to give you that option. Books that have happy endings sell. We all love the story about the kid who "beat the odds." The reality is, most kids do not beat the odds, and we have to stop accepting the social conditions in this country that put large numbers of children at risk. I know that sounds preachy; that is just my opinion.

14

Broken Three Times

LESSONS LEARNED

Broken Promises.
Baby you won't be gone long. I'm gonna do what I gotta do so you can come home.

Broken Spirits.
I am tired all the time. I feel like I am an inch from death.

Broken Child Welfare System.
The placement fell through partly due to poor scheduling of a much needed meeting and lack of communication.

What are the lessons we have learned from the telling of this family's story?

#1: Repeat placement changes take an enormous toll

Recently when meeting with Samya, she said to me, "If we stayed with the Olsens, our lives would really have been on track." She is probably right.

It is incredible what we ask children in the child welfare system to do. We drop them off on a stranger's doorstep at nine o'clock at night, and expect them to wake up the next morning, travel up to an hour to school, and carry on through their normal school day with business as usual.

After the passing of the Adoption and Safe Families Act in 1997, and the push for states to move children from long-term foster care to adoption, I once had a worker call me and ask for a clinical update for paperwork she was preparing to locate a new home for this one child. I was surprised, because the eight-year-old girl had been in this couple's home since she was six months old, and last I heard, there were no problems. The worker concurred there were no problems, but she was trying to find this girl a "permanent" home, and given that the couple was in their sixties and not interested in adopting, she was looking for a new home for this girl.

Permanence can be legal, or it can be psychological. The couple was willing to make a lifelong commitment to the child, but did not want to adopt her so she would remain eligible for health care and education benefits, that at that time, she would have lost if she were adopted. When I first started talking about the reasons the girl should not be moved, the worker said to me, "Children move all the time."

It has been almost two decades since that conversation; I am hopeful this worker and others in the field would no longer make a statement like that. Strong data show that continuity in placements and relationships is critical. As we saw when the children were first placed with the Olsens, they showed a remarkable capacity for recovery; with each added loss and adversity, their capacity to bounce back diminished. The uphill climb facing Sylar and Samya today is steeper than it needed to be.

#2: Discontinuity in caseworkers compromises casework practice

When Carly (DCF-W6) was trying to find a place for the children to stay after they were removed precipitously from the Olsen's home, Carly learned for the first time that there was an incident of sexual acting out behavior that happened when Sylar was at the Safe Home. She had not known about it, and neither had Sylar's therapist Dr. Worth. In being asked to make a placement recommendation, in light of this new information Dr. Worth suggested, "It might be best to err on the side of caution and place Sylar in a home with only males and with no children less than twelve. That will reduce the risk of anything happening."

After being removed from the Olsen home, Sylar moved five times over a five-week period of time, because no homes could be found that met those criteria. Would Sylar have been referred for mental health counseling and a psychosexual evaluation in a more timely fashion if there were greater continuity in workers? Could the five moves have been prevented? Or more importantly, if there were greater continuity in workers, and a stronger relationship between the worker and the Olsens, and the worker and the children, could the children's removal from the Olsen's home have been prevented altogether? There are data to suggest that this is likely.

Throughout the story there were countless examples of DCF staff going above and beyond the call of duty, as when Shannon picked up cupcakes for Samya's birthday, when Monica (DCF-W7) stopped off after hours at Tori's house, and when the on-call worker who met Samya at the ER gave Samya her phone number and said Samya could call anytime she needed someone to talk to. Samya never took that worker up on her offer, as she had never met her before, and never saw her again. Lifelines are built through continuity, not intermittent random acts of kindness.

Issues of staff turnover and workforce development are at the forefront of child welfare reform efforts, and critical to the maintenance of the gains made in the system, and ongoing improvement in child welfare practice.[149] For additional resources on this topic, the interested reader is referred to Reference 149.

#3: Casework practice is also compromised by inadequate use of case history contained in the records

Are there New York State records that were not shared with Connecticut pertaining to Sylar's allegations of being prostituted by his mother? We may never know.

Would DCF-1 have concluded her investigation differently if she had obtained the records from New York describing the situation with Gregory and concerns about Maria's recent drug use?

Would Samya have stabilized after seeing Joseph at the party at Tori's niece's house if Monica (DCF-W7) had known who Joseph was?

For our research in Vermont, we pull the child maltreatment reports for all investigations involving the children in the study. I remember the first year I was working in Vermont having a worker say to me, "I had no idea [child's name] had so many reports." Despite the fact that investigation reports are computerized in most states, in my experience, it is not standard practice for workers to review all prior reports when assigned a case that is re-referred for new allegations of abuse or neglect.

I once had a worker in Connecticut call me to ask about a child in our research who was recently removed from her father's care due to allegations of physical abuse. She let me know that she was planning on placing the child and her siblings with their birth mother, who had told the worker she had voluntarily given the kids to their father so she could go back to school. I let the worker know that the mother did *not* voluntarily give the children to their father; DCF, the agency she works for, had placed them with their father a year and a half earlier after mom went on a four-day drug binge and left the four children alone to fend for themselves.

Far too often each new referral is evaluated tabula rasa. Protocols need to be developed to assure case history is always thoroughly reviewed and incorporated into the treatment planning and ongoing management of every case.

#4: Although there have been noteworthy advances in the field, there are no panaceas when it comes to treating mental health, addiction, and family violence

Maria has multiple family members with a history of drug problems, and she likely has a genetic predisposition for addiction. She experienced repeated sexual assaults throughout her childhood for over a decade, and also experienced an inordinate amount of trauma in her adult life. She has had a lot of treatment over the years, and continues on psychotropic medication. Although she had a brief multiyear period of sobriety, she is once again actively suffering with an addiction disorder.

As discussed in the preface for this book, no treatment in psychiatry works for all patients, and individuals with a history of early childhood trauma are more likely to have a protracted course of illness and be less responsive to evidence-based treatments. Through translational research studies—insights from animal studies that have application in humans—we are beginning to unravel the mechanisms by which early adversity confers risk for psychiatric illnesses, substance use disorders, and a whole host of other health problems. We are learning more about the effects of early stress on gene regulation and brain development, delineating sensitive periods of development—times in development when individuals are more sensitive to both the positive and negative influences in the environment—and starting to learn how to expand the windows of sensitivity to enhance the likelihood of positive outcomes. It is the hope that through these ongoing multidisciplinary efforts, we will learn how to increase the odds of recovery for individuals like Maria who are at the highest risk for long-term deleterious outcomes.

#5 Barriers between service systems impede the delivery of effective multifaceted interventions to meet the diverse needs of parents and children involved with child welfare

The service needs of children and families involved with child welfare are diverse, yet very few service agencies can provide adult and child mental health services or mental health and addiction interventions, let alone physical health care, child and adult mental health services, addiction treatment, and all the auxiliary (e.g., housing, education, job training, case management) supports necessary to meet the needs of many of the families who come to the attention of the child welfare system.

In a step toward this goal, states across the country are promoting integrated physical and behavioral health care delivery as part of their efforts to deliver high-quality, cost-effective care to Medicaid beneficiaries with comorbid physical and behavioral health conditions.[150] The Medicaid expansion authorized by the Affordable Care Act brings greater import to these efforts, as millions of uninsured low-income adults, many with behavioral health conditions, gain coverage and states are required to provide behavioral health services to meet federal parity laws. To accomplish this, states are exploring ways to eliminate system-level impediments to the delivery of integrated care by revising their administrative, purchasing, financing, and regulatory structures.[150] The interested reader is referred to Reference 150 for a report on the strategies states are deploying to address or eliminate system-level barriers to integrated behavioral health and medical health care service delivery. This provides an excellent model to begin to address the integration of the broader array of service systems relevant for providing an even greater multifaceted integrated level of care for families involved with child welfare.

6 Every child needs a family. This is true for young children and teens within the child welfare system

As a graduate student in psychology at Yale, one of my mentors, Dr. Al Solnit said to me, "All the best professionals does not one good parent make." That is a phrase that always stuck with me and guided my clinical work with children over the years. The same message had been delivered to me earlier by a special education teacher who was supervising me in my first practicum as an undergraduate when I worked at a day treatment program operated by Tufts New England Medical Center for maltreated children. She advised me to always be conscious of the boundaries of my role, and reminded me that when one of the children in our class woke up in the middle the night with a nightmare, we wouldn't be there. Every child deserves a responsible, stable, caring adult to be there at those times, and for all those other special moments throughout life that call for a parent or parent-figure. I have a 22- year-old and a 19-year-old. Despite their many advantages in life, neither of them would be ready to navigate this world entirely on their own.

Children need families for a lifetime. Whenever possible, children should be with their birth families, and our best efforts should be made to support parents in this role. When this is not possible, kinship care should be explored, and if that is not feasible, alternate long-term substitute families provided. As reiterated throughout this book, the availability of a positive stable supportive caregiver is the most important factor in promoting resilience in maltreated children.

Recently, when I provided some small material support for Sylar, he said to me, "You've been more of a mother to me than my own mother." When he said this, it made vividly clear how profoundly the system had failed him.

REFERENCES

1. Kaufman J, Zigler E. Do abused children become abusive parents? *Am J Orthopsychiatry*. 1987;57(2):186–192.
2. Harris M, Fallot RD, eds. *Using Trauma Theory to Design Service Systems*. San-Francisco: Jossey-Bass; 2001.
3. National Child Traumatic Stress Network (NCTSN). Trauma-Informed Child Welfare Toolkit. In: Families NCTSNCCfCa, Ed. *Using a Trauma-Informed Lens to Help Transform the Child Welfare System*. San Diego, CA: Author. 2013;http://www.surveygizmo.com/s3/1211760/Access-to-the-Trauma-Informed-Child-Welfare-Practice-Toolkit.
4. Thrive Initiative. Thrive: Maine's Trauma-Informed System of Care Final Evaluation Report 2012; http://thriveinitiative.org/thrive-maines-trauma-informed-system-of-care-final-evaluation-report/.
5. Schaefer M. Public Sector Behavioral Health for Children and Families: Aligning Systems and Incentives. Zigler Center in Child Development and Social Policy Colloquium Series; November, 9, 2007. New Haven, CT: Zigler Center; 2007.
6. Gruendel J. *Young Children and Inpatient Care: An Analysis of HUSKY Data*. Rocky Hill, CT: 2013, Department of Children and Families, State of Connecticut, unpublished report.
7. Cohen JA, Deblinger E, Mannarino AP, Steer RA. A multisite, randomized controlled trial for children with sexual abuse-related PTSD symptoms. *J Am Acad Child Adolesc Psychiatry*. 2004;43(4):393–402.
8. Nanni V, Uher R, Danese A. Childhood maltreatment predicts unfavorable course of illness and treatment outcome in depression: a meta-analysis. *Am J Psychiatry*. 2012;169(2):141–151.
9. Teicher MH, Samson JA. Childhood maltreatment and psychopathology: A case for ecophenotypic variants as clinically and neurobiologically distinct subtypes. *Am J Psychiatry*. 2013;170(10):1114–1133.
10. Administration on Children, Youth and Families, Children's Bureau, U.S. Department of Health and Human Services. *Child Maltreatment 2004*. Washington, DC: U.S. Government Printing Office; 2006.
11. Administration on Children, Youth and Families. Children's Bureau, U.S. Department of Health and Human Services. *Child Maltreatment 2013*. 2015; http://www.acf.hhs.gov/sites/default/files/cb/cm2013.pdf
12. Drake B, Jonson-Reid M, Way I, Chung S. Substantiation and recidivism. *Child Maltreat*. 2003;8(4):248–260.
13. Gateway CWI. *Differential Response to Reports of Child Abuse*. Washington, DC: Department of Health and Human Services, Children's Bureau; 2014.
14. Kyte A, Trocme N, Chamberland C. Evaluating where we're at with differential response. *Child Abuse Negl*. 2013;37(2-3):125–132.

15. Casey Family Programs. Comparison of Experiences in Differential Response (DR) Implementation: 10 Child Welfare Jurisdictions Implementing DR. 2012; http://www.casey.org/differential-response-implementation/.

16. Loman LA, Siegel GL. Effects of approach and services under differential response on long term child safety and welfare. *Child Abuse Negl.* 2015;39:86–97.(doi):10.1016/j.chiabu.2014.1005.1014. Epub 2014 Jun 21.

17. Hughes RC, Rycus JS, Saunders-Adams SM, Hughes LK, Hughes KN. Issues in Differential Response. *Res Soc Work Pract.* 2013;23(5):493–520.

18. Hughes RC, Rycus JS. Discussion of issues in Differential Response. *Res Soc Work Pract.* 2013;5(23):563–577.

19. Vaughan-Eden V, Vandervort FE. Invited commentary on "Issues in Differential Response." *Res Soc Work Pract.* 2013;23(5):550–553.

20. Sheldon-Sherman J, Wilson D, Smith S. Extent and nature of child maltreatment-related fatalities: implications for policy and practice. *Child Welfare.* 2013;92(2):41–58.

21. Leventhal JM, Gaither JR. Incidence of serious injuries due to physical abuse in the United States: 1997 to 2009. *Pediatrics.* 2012;130(5):e847–e852.

22. Oliveros A, Kaufman J. Addressing substance abuse treatment needs of parents involved with the child welfare system. *Child Welfare.* 2011;90(1):25–41.

23. National Center on Substance Abuse and Child Welfare (NCSACW). http://www.ncsacw.samhsa.gov.

24. Young NK, Gardner SL. *Navigating the Pathways: Lessons and Promising Practices in Linking Alcohol and Drug Services with Child Welfare.* Technical Assistance Publication (TAP) Series. Rockville, MD: U.S. Department of Health and Human Services. Substance Abuse and Mental Health Services Administration. Center for Substance Abuse Treatment; 2002.

25. Schaeffer CM, Swenson CC, Tuerk EH, Henggeler SW. Comprehensive treatment for co-occurring child maltreatment and parental substance abuse: Outcomes from a 24-month pilot study of the MST-Building Stronger Families program. *Child Abuse Negl.* 2013;37(8):596–607.

26. Swenson CC, Schaeffer CM, Tuerk EH, et al. Adapting Multisystemic Therapy for Co-Occurring Child Maltreatment and Parental Substance Abuse: The Building Stronger Families Project. *Emotional & Behavioral Disorders in Youth.* 2009;Winter:3–8.

27. Wood E, Samet JH, Volkow ND. Physician education in addiction medicine. *JAMA.* 2013;310(16):1673–1674.

28. O'Brien CP. Anticraving medications for relapse prevention: a possible new class of psychoactive medications. *Am J Psychiatry.* 2005;162(8):1423–1431.

29. Shen XY, Orson FM, Kosten TR. Vaccines against drug abuse. *Clin Pharmacol Ther.* 2012;91(1):60–70.

30. Nestler EJ. Epigenetic mechanisms of drug addiction. *Neuropharmacology.* 2014;76 Pt B:259–268.

31. DeSena AD, Murphy RA, Douglas-Palumberi H, et al. SAFE Homes: Is it worth the cost? An evaluation of a group home permanency planning program for children who first enter out-of-home care. *Child Abuse Negl.* 2005;29:627–643.

32. Watts C, Zimmerman C. Violence against women: global scope and magnitude. *Lancet.* 2002;359(9313):1232–1237.

33. Tjaden P, Thoennes N. *Full Report of the Prevalence, Incidence, and Consequences of Violence Against Women: Research Report*. Washington, DC: U.S. Department of Justice; 2000.

34. Millett LS, Seay KD, Kohl PL. A national study of intimate partner violence risk among female caregivers involved in the child welfare system: The role of nativity, acculturation, and legal status. *Child Youth Serv Rev*. 2015;48:60–69.

35. Grasso D, Boonsiri J, Lipschitz D, et al. Posttraumatic stress disorder: the missed diagnosis. *Child Welfare*. 2009;88(4):157–176.

36. Babcock JC, Green CE, Robie C. Does batterers' treatment work? A meta-analytic review of domestic violence treatment. *Clin Psychol Rev*. 2004;23(8):1023–1053.

37. Feder L, Wilson DB. A meta-analytic review of courtmandated batterer intervention programs: Can courts affect abusers' behavior?. *Journal of Experimental Criminology*. 2005;1:239–262.

38. Stover CS, Meadows A, Kaufman J. Interventions for intimate partner violence: Review and implications for evidence-based practice. *Prof Psychol: Res Pr*. 2009;40(3):223–233.

39. Miller S. Discussing the Duluth Curriculum: creating a process of change for men who batter. *Violence Against Women*. 2010;16(9):1007–1021.

40. Easton CJ, Mandel DL, Hunkele KA, Nich C, Rounsaville BJ, Carroll KM. A cognitive behavioral therapy for alcohol-dependent domestic violence offenders: an integrated substance abuse–domestic violence treatment approach (SADV). *Am J Addict*. 2007;16(1):24–31.

41. Fals-Stewart W, Klostermann K, Yates BT, O'Farrell TJ, Birchler GR. Brief relationship therapy for alcoholism: a randomized clinical trial examining clinical efficacy and cost-effectiveness. *Psychol Addict Behav*. 2005;19(4):363–371.

42. Lam WK, Fals-Stewart W, Kelley ML. Effects of Parent Skills Training with Behavioral Couples Therapy for alcoholism on children: a randomized clinical pilot trial. *Addict Behav*. 2008;33(8):1076–1080.

43. Lam WK, Fals-Stewart W, Kelley ML. Parent training with behavioral couples therapy for fathers' alcohol abuse: effects on substance use, parental relationship, parenting, and CPS involvement. *Child Maltreat*. 2009;14(3):243–254.

44. Stover CS. Fathers for Change for Substance Use and Intimate Partner Violence: Initial Community Pilot. *Family Process*. 2015;54:1–10.

45. George DT, Phillips MJ, Lifshitz M, et al. Fluoxetine treatment of alcoholic perpetrators of domestic violence: a 12-week, double-blind, randomized, placebo-controlled intervention study. *J Clin Psychiatry*. 2011;72(1):60–65.

46. National Resource Center on Domestic Violence (NRCDV). http://www.nrcdv.org/.

47. Klasen M, Zvyagintsev M, Schwenzer M, et al. Quetiapine modulates functional connectivity in brain aggression networks. *Neuroimage*. 2013;75:20–26.

48. Burns B, Phillips S, Wagner H, et al. Mental health need and access to mental health services by youths involved with child welfare: a national survey. *J Am Acad Child Adolesc Psychiatry*. 2004;43(8):960–970.

49. Garland AF, Lau AS, Yeh M, McCabe KM, Hough RL, Landsverk JA. Racial and ethnic differences in utilization of mental health services among high-risk youths. *Am J Psychiatry*. 2005;162(7):1336–1343.

50. Wells R, Hillemeier MM, Bai Y, Belue R. Health service access across racial/ethnic groups of children in the child welfare system. *Child Abuse Negl*. 2009;33(5):282–292.

51. Cross TL. Disproportionality in child welfare. *Child Welfare*. 2008;87(2):11–20.

52. Semanchin Jones A. Implementation of Differential Response: a racial equity analysis. *Child Abuse Negl*. 2015;39:73–85. (doi):10.1016/j.chiabu.2014.1004.1013. Epub 2014 Jun 1012.

53. Administration on Children, Youth and Families. *Child Maltreatment 2007*. Washington, DC: U.S. Department of Health and Human Services; 2009.

54. Magruder J, Shaw TV. Children ever in care: an examination of cumulative disproportionality. *Child Welfare*. 2008;87(2):169–188.

55. Farber J, Bensky L, Alpert L. *The Long Road Home: A Study of Children Stranded in New York City Foster Care*. New York, New York; Children's Rights; 2009.

56. Drake B, Jolley JM, Lanier P, Fluke J, Barth RP, Jonson-Reid M. Racial bias in child protection? A comparison of competing explanations using national data. *Pediatrics*. 2011;127(3):471–478.

57. Miller OA, Ward KJ. Emerging strategies for reducing racial disproportionality and disparate outcomes in child welfare: the results of a national breakthrough series collaborative. *Child Welfare*. 2008;87(2):211–240.

58. Annie E. Casey Foundation (AECF). Places to Watch: Promising Practices to Address Racial Disproportionality in Child Welfare. 2005; http://www.cssp.org/publications/child-welfare/top-five/places-to-watch-promising-practices-to-address-racial-disproportionality-in-child-welfare.pdf.

59. Taylor AL. The African American Heart Failure Trial: a clinical trial update. *Am J Cardiol*. 2005;96(7B):44–48.

60. Administration on Children, Youth and Families. Child Welfare Outcomes 2009–2012: Report to Congress. 2014; http://www.acf.hhs.gov/sites/default/files/cb/cwo09_12.pdf, 2015.

61. James S. Why do foster care placements disrupt? An investigation of reasons for placement change in foster care. *Soc Serv Rev*. 2004;78(4):601–627.

62. Pecora P, Kessler R, Williams J, et al. *Improving Family Foster Care: Findings from the Northwest Foster Care Alumni Study*. Seattle, WA: Casey Family Programs; 2005.

63. Courtney JR, Prophet R. Predictors of placement stability at the state level: the use of logistic regression to inform practice. *Child Welfare*. 2011;90(2):127–142.

64. Leve LD, Harold GT, Chamberlain P, Landsverk JA, Fisher PA, Vostanis P. Practitioner review: Children in foster care—vulnerabilities and evidence-based interventions that promote resilience processes. *J Child Psychol Psychiatry*. 2012;53(12):1197–1211. http://www.ncbi.nlm.nih.gov/pmc/articles/PMC3505234/pdf/nihms3394946.pdf.

65. Newton RR, Litrownik AJ, Landsverk JA. Children and youth in foster care: distangling the relationship between problem behaviors and number of placements. *Child Abuse Negl*. 2000;24(10):1363–1374.

66. Dozier M, Lindhiem O. This is my child: differences among foster parents in commitment to their young children. *Child Maltreat*. 2006;11(4):338–345.

67. Jones AS, Wells SJ. *PATH/Wisconsin—Bremer Project: Preventing Placement Disruptions in Foster Care*. University of Minnesota: Center for Advanced Studies in Child Welfare. 2008; http://cascw.umn.edu/wp-content/uploads/2013/12/Path_BremerReport.pdf, 2015.

68. Shafer S. Child Welfare Permanency Mediation. *Child Welfare Court Improvement Project*. 2002; https://www.nycourts.gov/ip/cwcip/Videos/Perm-Mediation/perm-mediation-transcript.pdf, 2015.

69. Baker AJ, Schneiderman M, Parker R. A survey of problematic sexualized behaviors of children in the New York City Child Welfare System: estimates of problem, impact on services, and need for training. *J Child Sex Abus*. 2001;10(4):67–80.

70. Friedrich WN., Grambsch P, Damon L, et al. Child Sexual Behavior Inventory: Normative and clinical comparisons. *Psychol Assess*. 1992;4(3):303–311.

71. Baker AJ, Gries L, Schneiderman M, Parker R, Archer M, Friedrich B. Children with problematic sexualized behaviors in the child welfare system. *Child Welfare*. 2008;87(1):5–27.

72. Vizard E. Practitioner review: The victims and juvenile perpetrators of child sexual abuse—assessment and intervention. *J Child Psychol Psychiatry*. 2013;54(5):503–515.

73. Ryan EP, Hunter JA, Murrie DC. *Juvenile Sex Offenders: A Guide to Evaluation and Treatment for Mental Health Professionals*. New York, NY: Oxford University Press; 2012.

74. Ravitz A. Review of Juvenile Sex Offenders: A Guide to Evaluation and Treatment for Mental Health Professionals. *J Child Adolesc Psychopharmacol*. 2015;25(5):454–455.

75. Fallon B, Trocme N, Fluke J, MacLaurin B, Tonmyr L, Yuan YY. Methodological challenges in measuring child maltreatment. *Child Abuse Negl*. 2010;34(1):70–79.

76. Finkelhor D, Shattuck A, Turner HA, Hamby SL. The lifetime prevalence of child sexual abuse and sexual assault assessed in late adolescence. *J Adolesc Health*. 2014;55(3):329–333.

77. Radford L, Corral S, Bradley C, et al. *Child Abuse and Neglect in the UK Today*. London; National Society for the Prevention of Cruelty to Children, 2011.

78. Reitzel LR, Carbonell JL. The effectiveness of sexual offender treatment for juveniles as measured by recidivism: a meta-analysis. *Sex Abuse*. 2006;18(4):401–421.

79. Letourneau EJ, Henggeler SW, Borduin CM, et al. Multisystemic therapy for juvenile sexual offenders: 1-year results from a randomized effectiveness trial. *J Fam Psychol*. 2009;23(1):89–102.

80. Letourneau EJ, Henggeler SW, McCart MR, Borduin CM, Schewe PA, Armstrong KS. Two-year follow-up of a randomized effectiveness trial evaluating MST for juveniles who sexually offend. *J Fam Psychol*. 2013;27(6):978–985.

81. Pullman L, Seto MC. Assessment and treatment of adolescent sexual offenders: implications of recent research on generalist versus specialist explanations. *Child Abuse Negl*. 2012;36(3):203–209.

82. Cohen JA, Mannarino AP. A treatment study for sexually abused preschool children: Outcome during a one-year follow-up. *J Am Acad Child Adolesc Psychiatry*. 1997;36(9):1228–1235.

83. Hunter J. Prolonged exposure treatment of chronic PTSD in juvenile sex offenders: promising results from two case studies. *Child Youth Care Forum*. 2010;39:367–384.

84. Friedrich WN, Baker AJ, Parker R, Schneiderman M, Gries L, Archer M. Youth with problematic sexualized behaviors in the child welfare system: a one-year longitudinal study. *Sex Abuse*. 2005;17(4):391–406.

85. Bureau Cs. Definitions of Child Abuse and Neglect: State Statutes Current through June 2014. *Child Welfare Information Gateway*. 2014; https://www.childwelfare.gov/pubPDFs/define.pdf.

86. End All Corporal Punishment of Children. Corporal Punishment of Children in the USA. *Global Initiative to End All Corporal Punishment of Children.* 2014; http://www.endcorporalpunishment.org/pages/pdfs/states-reports/USA.pdf.

87. Office of Children and Family Services. *New York State: Children Allegedly Abused or Neglected by Foster Parents.* New York, NY: Author; 2013; http://nysccc.org/wp-content/uploads/AllegationsData.pdf.

88. Euser S, Alink LR, Tharner A, van IJzendoorn J. Out of home placement to promote safety? The prevalence of physical abuse in residential and foster care. *Child Youth Serv Rev.* 2014;37:64–70.

89. Euser S, Alink LR, Tharner A, van Ijzendoorn MH, Bakermans-Kranenburg MJ. The prevalence of child sexual abuse in out-of-home care: a comparison between abuse in residential and in foster care. *Child Maltreat.* 2013;18(4):221–231.

90. Laws R. False Abuse Allegations: Part 2. What Parents Can Do: A Checklist. 2002; http://www.adopting.org/adoptions/false-abuse-allegations-adoption-and-foster-care-by-rita-laws-phd-what-parents-can-do-a-checklist.html.

91. New York State Citizens Coalition for Children (NYSCCC). False Allegations of Abuse/Neglect. 2015; http://nysccc.org/fostercare/legal-issues/abuseneglect-allegations/.

92. Martin-Hushman D. North American Council on Adoptable Children. Allegations happen: how to prevent and survive them. *Adoptalk.*Spring 2002; http://www.nacac.org/adoptalk/allegations.html.

93. Kaufman J. Depressive disorders in maltreated children. *J Am Acad Child Adolesc Psychiatry.* 1991;30(2):257–265.

94. Kaufman J, Yang BZ, Douglas-Palumberi H, et al. Brain-derived neurotrophic Factor-5-HTTLPR gene interactions and environmental modifiers of depression in children. *Biol Psychiatry.* 2006;59:673–680.

95. Kaufman J, Yang BZ, Douglas-Palumberi H, et al. Social supports and serotonin transporter gene moderate depression in maltreated children. *Proc Natl Acad Sci U S A.* 2004;101(49):17316–17321.

96. Caspi A, Sugden K, Moffitt TE, et al. Influence of life stress on depression: moderation by a polymorphism in the 5-HTT gene. *Science.* 2003;301:386–389.

97. Karg K, Burmeister M, Shedden K, Sen S. The serotonin transporter promoter variant (5-HTTLPR), stress, and depression meta-analysis revisited: evidence of genetic moderation. *Arch Gen Psychiatry.* 2011;68(5):444–454.

98. Aslund C, Leppert J, Comasco E, Nordquist N, Oreland L, Nilsson KW. Impact of the interaction between the 5HTTLPR polymorphism and maltreatment on adolescent depression. A population-based study. *Behav Genet.* 2009;39(5):524–531.

99. Szyf M. The early life environment and the epigenome. *Biochem Biophys Acta.* 2009;1790(9):878–885.

100. Zhang TY, Meaney MJ. Epigenetics and the environmental regulation of the genome and its function. *Annu Rev Psychol.* 2010;61:439–466, C431–C433.

101. Kaufman J, Weder N. Neurobiology of early life stress: evolving concepts. In: Martin A, Scahill L, Kratochvil CJ, eds. *Pediatric Psychopharmacology.* 2nd ed. New York, NY: Oxford University Press; 2010:112–123.

102. Carrion VG, Wong SS. Can traumatic stress alter the brain? Understanding the implications of early trauma on brain development and learning. *J Adolesc Health.* 2012;51(Suppl 2):S23–S28. doi: 10.1016/j.jadohealth.2012.1004.1010.

103. Kaffman A, Meaney MJ. Neurodevelopmental sequelae of postnatal maternal care in rodents: clinical and research implications of molecular insights. *J Child Psychol Psychiatry.* 2007;48(3–4):224–244.

104. Tyrka AR, Burgers DE, Philip NS, Price LH, Carpenter LL. The neurobiological correlates of childhood adversity and implications for treatment. *Acta Psychiatr Scand.* 2013;128(6):434–447.

105. Kaufman J, Plotsky P, Nemeroff C, Charney D. Effects of early adverse experience on brain structure and function: clinical implications. *Biol Psychiatry.* 2000;48(8):778–790.

106. McGowan PO, Sasaki A, D'Alessio AC, et al. Epigenetic regulation of the glucocorticoid receptor in human brain associates with childhood abuse. *Nat Neurosci.* 2009;12(3):342–348.

107. Yang B-Z, Zhang H, Ge W, et al. Child abuse and epigenetic mechanisms of disease risk. *Am J Prev Medicine.* 2013;44(2):101–107.

108. Curley JP, Jensen CL, Mashoodh R, Champagne FA. Social influences on neurobiology and behavior: epigenetic effects during development. *Psychoneuroendocrinology.* 2011;36(3):352–371.

109. Nestler EJ. Epigenetic mechanisms in psychiatry. *Biol Psychiatry.* 2009;65(3):189–190.

110. Rutten BP, Mill J. Epigenetic mediation of environmental influences in major psychotic disorders. *Schizophr Bull.* 2009;35(6):1045–1056.

111. Felitti VJ, Anda RF, Nordenberg D, et al. Relationship of childhood abuse and household dysfunction to many of the leading causes of death in adults. The Adverse Childhood Experiences (ACE) Study. *Am J Prev Medicine.* 1998;14(4):245–258.

112. Larkin H, Felitti VJ, Anda RF. Social work and adverse childhood experiences research: implications for practice and health policy. *Soc Work Public Health.* 2014;29(1):1–16.

113. Weder N, Kaufman J. Critical periods revisited: implications for intervention with traumatized children. *J Am Acad Child Adolesc Psychiatry.* 2011;50(11):1087–1089; (http://www.ncbi.nlm.nih.gov/pmc/articles/PMC3758247/pdf/nihms3462427.pdf)

114. Turecki G, Ota V, Belangero S, Jackowski A, Kaufman J. Early life adversity, genomic plasticity, and psychopathology. *Lancet Psychiatry.* 2014;1(6):461–466.

115. Montalvo-Ortiz J, Gelernter J, Hudziak J, Kaufman J. RDoC and Translational Perspectives on the Genetics of Trauma-Related Psychiatric Disorders. *AmJ Med Genet: Neuropsychiatr Genet.* in press.

116. Davidson RJ, McEwen BS. Social influences on neuroplasticity: stress and interventions to promote well-being. *Nat Neurosci.* 2012;15(5):689–695.

117. Zima BT, Bussing R, Crecelius GM, Kaufman A, Belin TR. Psychotropic medication treatment patterns among school-aged children in foster care. *J Child Adolesc Psychopharmacol.* 1999;9(3):135–147.

118. dosReis S, Zito JM, Safer DJ, Soeken KL. Mental health services for youths in foster care and disabled youths. *Am J Public Health.* 2001;91(7):1094–1099.

119. Naylor MW, Davidson CV, Ortega-Piron DJ, Bass A, Gutierrez A, Hall A. Psychotropic medication management for youth in state care: consent, oversight, and policy considerations. *Child Welfare.* 2007;86(5):175–192.

120. Texas Health and Human Services Commission (THHSC). Use of Psychoactive Medication in Texas Foster Children, State Fiscal Year 2005. 2006; http://www.hhs.state.tx.us/news/release/Analysis 062306.pdf.

121. Zito JM, Safer DJ, Sai D, et al. Psychotropic medication patterns among youth in foster care. *Pediatrics.* 2008;121(1):e157–e163.

122. P.L.110-351. The Fostering Connections to Success and Increasing Adoptions Act of 2008. 2008.

123. P.L.112-34. The Child and Family Services Improvement and Innovation Act. 2011.

124. Administration for Children and Families (ACF). Use of Psychotropic Medications. 2012; https://www.childwelfare.gov/topics/systemwide/mentalhealth/effectiveness/psychotropic/?hasBeenRedirected=1.

125. Administration for Children and Families (ACF). Psychotropic Drug Use Policy Letter to State Agency Officials. 2011; http://www.medicaid.gov/Federal-Policy-Guidance/downloads/SMD-11-23-11.pdf.

126. ACF. Oversight of Psychotropic Medication for Children in Foster Care; Title IV-B Health Care Oversight & Coordination Plan. 2012; https://www.acf.hhs.gov/sites/default/files/cb/im1203.pdf.

127. Cohen JA, Mannarino AP, Perel JM, Staron V. A pilot randomized controlled trial of combined trauma-focused CBT and sertraline for childhood PTSD symptoms. *J Am Acad Child Adolesc Psychiatry.* 2007;46(7):811–819.

128. Famularo R, Kinscherff R, Fenton T. Propranolol treatment for childhood posttraumatic stress disorder, acute type. A pilot study. *Am J Dis Child.* 1988;142(11):1244–1247.

129. Scheeringa MS, Weems CF. Randomized placebo-controlled D-cycloserine with cognitive behavior therapy for pediatric posttraumatic stress. *J Child Adolesc Psychopharmacol.* 2014;24(2):69–77. doi: 10.1089/cap.2013.0106. Epub Feb 2014.

130. Birmaher B, Brent D, Bernet W, et al. Practice parameter for the assessment and treatment of children and adolescents with depressive disorders. *J Am Acad Child Adolesc Psychiatry.* 2007;46(11):1503–1526.

131. Anda RF, Brown DW, Dube SR, Bremner JD, Felitti VJ, Giles WH. Adverse childhood experiences and chronic obstructive pulmonary disease in adults. *Am J Prev Med.* 2008;34(5):396–403.

132. U.S. Department of Health and Human Services, Administration on Children, Youth and Families, Children's Bureau. *The AFCARS Report.* Washington, DC: Author; 2013.

133. Spitz RA. Hospitalism; an inquiry into the genesis of psychiatric conditions in early childhood. *Psychoanal Study Child.* 1945;1:53–74.

134. United Nations General Assembly (UNGA). *Convention on the Rights of the Child, United Nations, Treaty Series.* UNGA; 1989.

135. United Nations General Assembly. *Guidelines for the Alternative Care of Children: Resolution. Adopted by the General Assembly.* UNGA; 2010.

136. Dozier M, Kaufman J, Kobak R, et al. Consensus statement on group care for children and adolescents: A statement of policy of the American Orthopsychiatric Association. *Am J Orthopsychiatry.* 2014;84(3):219–225.

137. Kerr DC, DeGarmo DS, Leve LD, Chamberlain P. Juvenile justice girls' depressive symptoms and suicidal ideation 9 years after Multidimensional Treatment Foster Care. *J Consult Clin Psychol.* 2014;82(4):684–693.

138. Winters KC, Botzet AM, Fahnhorst T. Advances in adolescent substance abuse treatment. *Curr Psychiatry Rep.* 2011;13(5):416–421.

139. Ryan JP, Marshall J, Herz D, Hernandez P. Juvenile delinquency in child welfare: Investigating group home effects. *Child Youth Serv Rev.* 2008;30:1088–1099.

140. Alink LRA, Euser S, Bakermans-Kranenburg MJ, van IJzendoorn, HM. A challenging job: Physical and sexual violence towards group workers in youth residential care. *Child and Youth Care Forum.* 2014;43:243–250.

141. Annie E. Casey Foundation. *Rightsizing Congregate Care.* (http://192.168.1.1:8181/ http://www.aecf.org/m/resourcedoc/AECF-RightsizingCongregateCare-2009.pdf). Baltimore, MD: Author ; 2009.

142. U.S. Department of Health and Human Services, Administration on Children, Youth and Families, Children's Bureau. *The AFCARS Report.* Washington, DC: Author; 2014.

143. Eyster L, Oldmixon SL. State Policies to Help Youth Transition Out of Foster Care. 2007; http://www.nga.org/files/live/sites/NGA/files/pdf/0701YOUTH.PDF.

144. Jim Casey Youth Opportunities Initiative (JCYOI). 2015; http://www.jimcaseyyouth. org/.

145. Dworsky A, Napolitano L, Courtney M. Homelessness during the transition from foster care to adulthood. *Am J Public Health.* 2013;103 Suppl 2(2):S318–S323.

146. Jim Casey Youth Opportunities Initiative (JCYOI). Cost Avoidance: The Business Case for Investing In Youth Aging Out of Foster Care. 2013; http://www.jimcaseyyouth.org/sites/default/files/Cost Avoidance Issue Brief_EMBARGOED until May 6. pdf.

147. Courtney ME, Terao S, Bost N. *Midwest Evaluation of the Adult Functioning of Former Foster Youth: Conditions of Youth Preparing to Leave State Care.* Chapin Hall Center for Children at the University of Chicago; 2004.

148. Bureau Cs. John H. Chafee Foster Care Independence Program. 2012; http://www.acf. hhs.gov/programs/cb/resource/chafee-foster-care-program.

149. McCarthy M, Lawson KB, Dickinson N. National Child Welfare Workforce Institute. 2015; http://ncwwi.org/index.php/about-ncwwi/ncwwi-overview.

150. Bachrach D, Anthony S, Manatt AD, Phelps & Phillips, LLP. State Strategies For Integrating Physical and Behavioral Health Services in a Changing Medicaid Environment. 2014; http://www.commonwealthfund.org/~/media/files/publications/ fund-report/2014/aug/1767_bachrach_state_strategies_integrating_phys_behavioral_hlt_827.pdf.

INDEX

CPSIA information can be obtained
at www.ICGtesting.com
Printed in the USA
BVHW030013110121
597517BV00011B/84/J

9 780199 399154